In the Company of Prophets

Reflections on Joshua, Judges, Samuel & Kings

DR. MOSHE SOKOLOW

KODESH PRESS

In the Company of Prophets:
Reflections on Joshua, Judges, Samuel & Kings

© Moshe Sokolow 2021

Hardback ISBN: 978-1-947857-64-3
Paperback ISBN: 978-1-947857-63-6

All rights reserved. Except for brief quotations in printed reviews, no part of this publication may be reproduced, stored in a retrieval system, or transmitted in any form or by any means (printed, written, photocopied, visual, electronic, audio, or otherwise) without the prior permissions of the publisher.

Published & Distributed by

Kodesh Press L.L.C.
New York, NY
www.KodeshPress.com
kodeshpress@gmail.com

Table of Contents

Prologue 7
An Introduction to Nevi'im Rishonim 9
Joshua 17
Judges 49
First Samuel 79
Second Samuel 121
First Kings 159
Second Kings 193

Prologue

On behalf of 929 English and Yeshiva University Press, it is an honor to publish this collection of Dr. Moshe Sokolow's reflections and insights into every chapter of the Former Prophets, covering the books of Joshua, Judges, Samuel, and Kings. These pieces all originated as contributions to the 929 English site (929.org.il), and tens of thousands of readers around the world have learned these chapters along with Dr. Sokolow's analyses through the 929 community.

For millennia, Jews around the world have been connected to one another in an annual cycle through the Torah. The modern era has opened unprecedented possibilities for connectedness around all of Tanakh and all of the world. 929 English works to create a platform to enable such a global community of learners. A cutting-edge project dedicated to creating a world-wide Jewish conversation around issues that unite and divide us, anchored in or inspired by the 929 chapters in Tanakh, users engage with one chapter a day, encountering the entire Hebrew Bible over the course of a 3.5-year cycle of study. The site presents creative readings and pluralistic interpretations from a wide range of writers, artists, rabbis, educators, scholars, novelists, poets, politicians, students and more.

With this volume by Dr. Moshe Sokolow, we complement the robust offerings available on the digital platform with the first tangible book in the 929 Library. Dr. Sokolow, the Fanya Gottesfeld-Heller Professor of Jewish Education and Associate Dean of Azrieli Graduate School of Jewish Education and Administration, is a renowned Jewish educator and communal leader. As a teacher of teachers, an author and a dear friend and mentor of many individuals, Dr. Sokolow's impact on learners across the globe continues to grow. His insights, scholarship, and pedagogical eye make this a fitting debut volume, and we are proud to offer it to the reading public. Dip into its pages with your *havruta*, use it to prepare a lesson to friends or students, and follow along as Dr. Sokolow guides us through the timeless messages of Israel's ancient prophets.

Rabbi Dr. Adam Mintz – Director, 929 English
Shira Hecht-Koller, Esq. – Director of Education, 929 English
Rabbi Dr. Stuart Halpern – Senior Advisor to the Provost,
    Yeshiva University

An Introduction to Nevi'im Rishonim

Indeed, my Lord God does nothing without having revealed
His purpose to His servants the prophets. (Amos 3:7)

I. The Text

Jewish tradition divides the 24 books of Tanakh into three parts: Torah, Nevi'im (Prophets), and Ketuvim (Writings). Torah consists of the Five Books of Moses (often known by the Greek name Pentateuch); Nevi'im is subdivided into Nevi'im Rishonim (early: Joshua, Judges, Samuel, Kings) and Nevi'im Aharonim (late: Isaiah, Jeremiah, Ezekiel, the Twelve, a.k.a., Minor, Prophets); and Ketuvim contains those designated Gedolim (large: Psalms, Proverbs, Job) and those called Ketanim (small: Five Megillot—Song of Songs, Ruth, Lamentations, Ecclesiastes, Esther—Daniel, Ezra-Nehemiah, and Chronicles).

The division between the "early" and "late" Prophets (albeit not, per se, talmudic[1]) can be justified on grounds of both form and

---

1. The term *Nevi'im Rishonim* appears in the Mishnah (*Yoma* 5:2) in conjunction with what has come to be called the Foundation Stone that is ostensibly embedded on the site of the Temple's Holy of Holies:

> After the Ark had been taken away, there was a stone from the days of the earlier prophets, called *shtiyah*, three fingers above the ground, on which [the *kohein*] would place [the pan of burning coals].

While edifying, this does not help to define either the prophets themselves or their chronological era more precisely.

content. The former books are overwhelmingly narrative prose with few poetic passages, while the latter are largely poetic. The former prophets performed largely political and military functions; the latter issued words of rebuke, impending doom, or consolation.

The opening Mishnah in *Avot* relates these chronological divisions to the chain of Jewish tradition (*masorah*), declaring that "Moses received the Torah at Sinai and transmitted it to Joshua. Joshua [transmitted it] to the Elders, the Elders to the Prophets, and the Prophets transmitted it to the Men of the Grand Assembly." The Elders in question are those who assumed governance over Israel after Joshua's death and are described at the close of the Book of Joshua as those "who lived on after Joshua, and who had experienced all the deeds that the Lord had wrought for Israel" (24:31). By implication, the Elders would include the Judges whose deeds are narrated in the book of that name, and the era of the Prophets would begin with Samuel, whose mission was launched at the start of the book that bears his name. (The identities of the Men of the Grand Assembly remain relatively obscure, save for two things: first, by implication, they followed after the Prophets—the last of whom, Malachi, functioned at the very beginning of the Second Temple era—and, second, subsequent rabbinic tradition explicitly named the last prophets—Haggai, Zechariah, and Malachi—as members of that Assembly.)

II. The Medium: "929"

"929 English," like its Hebrew counterpart, is intent upon raising the prestige of Bible study by facilitating a daily encounter with biblical texts. Five times weekly, online access is provided to the Masoretic text, an English translation (courtesy of the Jewish Publication Society, via Sefaria), and an array of comments offered by scholars, rabbis, teachers, public figures, culture leaders, and even *"balabatim"* (ordinary folks) who have something worthwhile to contribute.

It is important to note that "929" readers are expected to read the biblical text (in Hebrew or translation) prior to consulting these comments, so there is little attempt here to provide either a synopsis of, or running commentary, on every chapter.

III. The Interpretation

There are essentially three basic forms that biblical interpretation may take: historical-philological, traditional-exegetical, and literary-critical. The first seeks to establish the meanings of words in the contexts in which they were first used and summons additional aid from the allied disciplines of comparative languages, literatures, and cultures, and from archaeology. The second seeks meaning via the traditions of the faith community that holds these ancient texts in such high regard that it refers to them as "Sacred Scripture." These range from the legal and narrative insights of the Talmud and Midrash, through the protean efforts of medieval exegetes such as Rashi, Ibn Ezra, Radak, and Ramban, and up to the contributions of such modern investigators as S.R. Hirsch, Malbim, and Nehama Leibowitz. The third approach, while not disregarding either of its two associates, focuses our attention on the literary styles in which biblical texts were written or redacted and utilizes many of the very methods of analysis that are used in literary studies in general.

It is my opinion that all three of the above approaches are valid, each addressing a distinctive dimension of Tanakh, and therefore the ideal way to study Tanakh is through a combination of all three.[2] However, because 929 essays are by design relatively short and discuss only selected verses, the somewhat indiscriminate nature of the insights collected here may obscure—or even distort—this prescription.

---

2. I have elaborated on this theory and freely illustrated it in a forthcoming book, *Pursuing Peshat: The Bible, Its Interpretation, and Religious Education*. In the interim, see "Authority and Validity, Why Tanakh Requires Interpretation and What Makes an Interpretation Legitimate?" *Meorot* 6:2 (2007), 1–14.

Nevertheless, examples of all three abound in this book, with those drawn from the realm of traditional exegesis taking pride of place.

IV. The Interpreter

My elementary school education in Tanakh (which, historically, has been the Jewish educational context in which Nevi'im Rishonim is studied) took place under very different pedagogical circumstances from those that prevail today. Many of my teachers, some of whom were Holocaust survivors, had been educated in Europe in a progressive religious school (*heder metukan*) whose curriculum was strong on Hebrew language (emphasizing grammar) and literature (Bialyk was a favorite). Tanakh, in their classes, was meant to be as much of an aesthetic experience as a spiritual one, and while I do not remember any specific interpretations they may have offered during our study, I can still recite by heart the numerous passages they had us memorize—from Joshua's lyric at Gibeon, to Deborah's victory song, to Hannah's song of thanksgiving, and on to David's ode to God at the close of his reign.

This *girsa d'yankuta* (childhood memorization) has played a prominent role in my lifelong attachment to Tanakh as well as frequently providing grist for the mill of original interpretation. My subsequent biblical and Semitic studies—at Yeshiva University and at other universities—coupled with my more recent preoccupation with the pedagogy of Tanakh,[3] have deepened this attachment as well as provided valuable diverse vantage points from which to view it.

Whenever I am asked what I get most out of the study of Tanakh, I like to reply by way of an anecdote that was shared with me by Moshe Zucker, one of my mentors, who, as a young man, had studied in the Rabbinical Seminary of Vienna. One day, the story goes, the seminarians all ganged up on the dean, Adolph Schwartz, a highly

---

3. See Moshe Sokolow, *TANAKH, An Owner's Manual* (NY: KTAV, 2015), particularly the chapter on "Tanakh and Pedagogy," 168ff.

regarded scholar himself, and demanded that he name for them—on the spot—the best commentary on the Bible. I leave you to ponder his reply: Jewish history.

Technicalities

All translations of biblical texts follow the *Jewish Publication Society Hebrew-English Tanakh* (1999), unless otherwise noted. Talmudic citations generally utilize the Soncino translation, and all other translations are original. The names of biblical characters appear in their accepted English formulations (e.g., Moses, Samuel), while those of post-biblical personalities use their standard Hebrew forms (e.g., Rabbi Moshe Feinstein, the Gaon Shmuel bar Hofni).

The title of the book is taken from 1 Samuel 19:20, which refers to *lahakat ha-nevi'im*. While the JPS translation is "a band of prophets," I prefer the King James version: "a company of prophets." The "929" experience has enabled its participants to share both the company of the Scriptural prophets as well as one another's company as they make their way through the biblical canon.

Acknowledgments

My thanks, first, to "929" English director, Adam Mintz (my Shabbat afternoon Gemara "rebbe"), its educational director, Shira Hecht-Koller, and its able managing editor, Jeremy Benstein. Gratitude is also due to Stuart Halpern and to Yeshiva University Press for extending its imprimatur, and to Alec Goldstein of Kodesh Press for his supervision of the editorial process.

On a more personal note, I am continually indebted to my wife, Judy, without whose discerning eye and felicitous pencil these remarks would be the poorer and this book but another ambition languishing on the shelf of unrealized aspirations.

I would like to dedicate this book to the generations fore and aft: my parents, Joseph and Hannah Sokolow, and in-laws, Sol and Roslyn

Sussman, all of blessed memory; our children, Shalom and his wife Sharon; and our grandchildren, Naomi and Rafi. May the words of the prophets ever be their lodestars, and may their deeds guide their own.

לולי תורתך שעשעי, אז אבדתי בעניי.
Moshe Sokolow
February 2021, Sh'vat 5781

Joshua

Benjamin West, *Joshua passing the River Jordan with the Ark of the Covenant* (1800)

Joshua 1

Big Shoes to Fill...

Moses, "servant (*'eved*) of God" (verse 1), is dead. He is succeeded by Joshua, who is rather pointedly described—by virtue of a nearly identical relationship—as: "Moses's servant (*mesharet*)" (ibid).

In verse 6, God tells Joshua to "be strong and resolute" (*hazak ve'ematz*) and adds, immediately thereafter (7), "Just be very strong and resolute (*raq hazak ve'ematz*). Rashi, troubled by the seemingly unnecessary repetition, distinguished between the two instructions. The first he interpreted as: "Be strong and resolute. In the physical sense, as it states: 'For you will lead this people to inherit the land.'" While the second he interpreted as: "Just be very strong and resolute. This was said in reference to the Torah, as it states: 'To preserve, to act in accordance with all the laws of the Torah.'"

The precedence which "the physical sense" takes over "the Torah" is reminiscent of the rabbinic adage: "Propriety precedes Torah" (*derekh eretz kadmah leTorah*). As much as the pursuit of Torah is the loftiest of all our possible objectives, our "lower-order needs" have to be met before our "higher-order needs" can be fulfilled, as Abraham Maslow reminded us in his well-known "hierarchy" (*A Theory of Human Motivation*). Hence, Joshua's very first instruction to Israel was: "Prepare food" (11).

The significance of "just be strong and resolute" is reinforced by the people's incorporation of the phrase in their inaugural declaration of loyalty to Joshua in the closing verse of our chapter: "Anyone who rebels against your instructions and disobeys anything that you command him, shall be put to death; just be strong and resolute" (*raq hazak ve'ematz*) (18).

Joshua 2

"I Spy"

There are both similarities between, and differences, regarding Joshua's mission to Jericho and the Torah's report on the earlier mission launched by Moses to scout the Land of Canaan (Numbers 12). The similarities speak for themselves: information of military and strategic value was required in each case and could be reliably secured only through the exercise of what has come to be known as "humint"—human intelligence. The differences, however, are striking.

Primarily, the scope was different. It required twelve scouts and forty days to complete the reconnaissance of the Land of Canaan, while only two spies and, arguably, only a few days were required for Jericho. It also appears that whereas the twelve scouts observed their objectives from afar (a recurring theme word in Numbers 12 is "we saw"), the two spies interacted with Rahab, their local source. Perhaps it is in consideration of this particular difference that the Torah defines the earlier mission as "scouting" (*latur et ha'aretz*) while Joshua's agents are clearly designated "spies" (*meraglim*).

Regarding the intelligence gathered, there is a remarkable agreement between the information conveyed to the spies by Rahab and an implicit assumption made earlier in the Torah. The song Israel sang after crossing the Red Sea states, "the entire population of Canaan melted (*namogu*). Fear and terror fell upon them" (Exodus 15:15–16). Rahab confirmed to the spies that "the fear of you has fallen upon us and the entire population has melted (*namogu*) before you" (Joshua 2:9). Small wonder, then, that of all they must have seen and heard during their mission, the words the spies chose to convey in their report to Joshua were "indeed, the entire population has melted (*namogu*) before us" (24).

Joshua 3

"The River Jordan is Chilly and Wide (Hallelujah)"

Joshua's crossing of the Jordan recalls Moses's crossing of the Red Sea in some respects and differs from it in others.

In both cases, the ordinary course of the water was interrupted to provide the opportunity to cross on dry land. A "ferocious easterly wind" that blew at the Red Sea all night (Exodus 14:21) caused "the flow to stand as still as a column" (*ned*), and in our chapter the Jordan's waters, too, "stood as still as a column" (*ned*) (16).

The interruptions, however, were initiated in dissimilar manners. While Moses (simply?) raised his arm and waved his staff, Joshua was instructed to send the priests bearing the Ark out into the Jordan. Only when "[their] feet are immersed in the water" (15) at the eastern bank of the river, did the waters stand still.

This distinction is somewhat reminiscent of a Midrash that credits Nahshon ben Aminadav with effecting the crossing of the Red Sea by being the first (and only?) person willing to risk entering it on the sole strength of God's assurance that it would split. Here, too, the priests had to immerse their own feet in the Jordan as a sign of their commitment to act solely on the strength of God's command.

And as the staff was a tangible reminder to Moses that he acted at God's behest, so had the Ark become, to the priests, the symbol of their dedication.

IN THE COMPANY OF PROPHETS

Joshua 4

A Levitating Ark?

At the close of the previous chapter, we left the priests immersed up to their feet in water on the eastern bank of the Jordan, waiting with the Ark while the rest of the people crossed over. When that crossing was complete, God instructed Joshua to have the priests "ascend from the Jordan" (16–17) and "as soon as the soles of the priests' feet were drawn up unto the dry ground, the waters of the Jordan returned to their place as before" (18).

To which "dry ground" were the priests' feet drawn up? While logic would have it that the reference is to the west bank of the Jordan—where the rest of the nation awaited them—a remarkable Midrash insists that the priests retreated to the eastern bank, whereupon "the Ark bore its bearers aloft and crossed."

Rabbi David Kimhi (Radak; Provence, 1160–1235), a critic of midrashic excess, wrote:

> I find this homily [*derash*] perplexing: What forced [the rabbis] into [this interpretation] of these verses? ... Even if we were to grant their premise, i.e., that the reference is to the bank of the Jordan whence they entered, [it would mean that] after all the people crossed, the ark followed them across to dry land, and when the feet of the *kohanim* were removed to the dry land *on the other* [western] *side* the waters resumed their course....
>
> What need is there to have the ark bear its bearers and cross? And if such a miracle did occur, would not the verse

have said [explicitly] that the ark bore its bearers aloft above the water?

Despite Radak's critique, this Midrash reprises itself apropos of 2 Samuel 6:6ff. When Uzzah reached out to prevent the Ark from slipping off the wagon transporting it back from the Philistines, God slew him. His crime, said Rashi: If the Ark could hold its bearers aloft, surely it needed no assistance to keep itself intact. (See our comments there.)

Joshua 5

Circumcision, Yes; Manna, Not Any More

Our chapter features two immediate consequences of the Israelites' entry into their own land. The first is the renewal of circumcision, and the other is the cessation of the manna. Both, while manifested physically, are essentially spiritual.

On the surface, Joshua's claim that the Israelites experienced mass circumcision prior to their departure from Egypt (5) appears to be baseless since no explicit reference is made to it in the Book of Exodus. From the perspective of traditional exegesis, however, it is implicit in what the Sages regarded as a process—akin to conversion—that also included immersion. As reported by Rambam (Maimonides):

> Israel entered into the covenant by way of three rites: circumcision, immersion, and sacrifice. Circumcision took place in Egypt.... Immersion took place in the wilderness before the revelation of the Torah... [as did the sacrifices]. (*Hilkhot Issurei Bi'ah* 13:1–3)

The manna, to recall, began to fall shortly after the crossing of the Red Sea and remained a fixture of the Israelites' diet throughout their sojourn in the wilderness. To cite Exodus 16:35: "The Children of Israel ate the manna for forty years, until they reached settled country; they ate manna until they came to the edge of the Land of Canaan." Now, almost immediately upon crossing the Jordan, they had arrived at that "edge," and the manna ceased to fall and was replaced by "the local produce" (12).

Throughout their divinely guided trek through the wilderness, the pillars of cloud and flame were adequate reminders of their elevated religious state. Now that they were entering the Land of Israel and were about to assume the responsibility for maintaining their own spirituality, they needed to resume circumcision as a sign of their particularity and replace the manna from heaven with the "seven species" for which the Land of Israel is praiseworthy.

Joshua 6

"And the Walls Came Tumbling Down"

One of the most striking features of the narrative of the fall of the walls and city of Jericho is the prominence of the number seven. Seven priests hold seven horns (vss. 4, 6, 8, 13) while circling the city on seven consecutive days, completing seven circuits on the seventh day (15). Traditionally, the number seven, being the number of days in a week, symbolizes the natural order, while eight, being in excess of seven, symbolizes something supernatural. (Hence, circumcision, which is clearly meant to supersede the natural order, takes place on the eighth day.)

That being the case, we might have expected the fall of Jericho to have been subject to the rule of eights since, presumably, it was miraculous. The prominence of seven, however, seems to indicate the opposite; from the perspective of the Book of Joshua it was accomplished within the natural order.

The ten plagues, the crossing of the Red Sea, the manna and quail in the wilderness, were all divine gifts that were bestowed upon a passive Israel as epitomized by the verse "The Lord will fight on your behalf while you remain silent" (Exodus 14:14). With the crossing of the Jordan and the entry into the Land of Israel, however, the people were now being actively entrusted with their own fate. In our comments on Chapter Three, we observed that unlike the Red Sea that split when Moses merely waved his staff over it, the priests bearing the Ark had to immerse their feet in the Jordan before it stopped flowing.

Now, as Israel approached its first military target, this new expectation continued. For six days, only the priests and the Ark participated. On the seventh day, the whole nation got involved. Of course, their shouting and horn blowing was insufficient, in itself, to cause the wall to fall down flat (20); but, on the other hand, it appears that without their contribution God would not have done it alone. They were being trained to take responsibility for their national destiny.

Joshua 7

Spoils of War… Spoil Wars

Taking spoils is generally permitted by the Torah. Indeed, we are bidden to "enjoy the spoils of your enemy which the Lord your God gives you" (Deut. 20:14). This enjoyment was practiced by the Israelites throughout the Biblical period, with a handful of notable prohibitions—one of which was Jericho. Their failure to observe this prohibition led to a most striking consequence: The very next military foray, at the city of Ai, projected to be a simple mission (3), failed, with the attendant deaths of 36 of the participating soldiers, because someone sinned, took the spoils, and then tried to cover it up.

A lottery identified the guilty party as member of the tribe of Judah named Achan (18), who confessed to his crime. Joshua, who had warned the people against the possible contamination by spoils (*'achartem*, 6:18), accused Achan of having done just that (*'achartanu*, 7:25). Achan was stoned to death, and the spoils were destroyed. The description of illegal spoils as a contaminant, however, has a curious epilogue. When the genealogy of the tribe of Judah is delineated in the Book of Chronicles, the name of the person who violated the ban against spoils is rendered as Achar, rather than Achan (1 Chron. 2:7), signifying that he had been completely redefined by this incident.

Another postscript, of sorts, attaches to the name that was given to the site at which the ill-gotten booty was burned: The people called it the "Valley of Contamination" (*'emek 'achor*, 26). According to the Prophet Hosea, that name was eventually going to be transformed into "The Gateway to Hope" (Hosea 2:17), in Hebrew: *Petah Tikvah*, and indeed it was, when early Zionist pioneers founded a settlement by that name in 1878.

Joshua 8

Joshua Pulls a "Moses"

Given that Ai had been reported by military intelligence to have a total population of 2,000 and to present no great threat (7:3–4), our chapter seemingly gives excessive coverage (29 verses!) to its eventual conquest. Did the lingering effects of the spoils scandal magnify its importance?

One detail of this conquest, however, summons up the recollection of a striking earlier victory. God instructed Joshua to reach out (*neteh*) with his spear towards Ai (8:19), which he kept extended until the victory was complete (26).

This effectively combines two poses of Moses into one: God's instruction him to reach out (*neteh*) with his staff in order to split the Red Sea, and his assumed stance during the battle against Amalek at Refidim, wherein he kept his arms extended all day until the battle was over (Exodus 17:11–12).

Two other subtler instances in our chapter link Joshua to Moses. In building an altar atop Mt. Ebal and conducting a public Torah reading, Joshua was clearly following the instructions of Deuteronomy (11:29ff.). And by removing the body of the King of Ai from the gallows at nightfall (29), he was honoring the Torah's prohibition against postmortem desecration (Deut. 21:23).

In delineating these similarities, the Book of Joshua is giving tangible evidence of God's earlier promise to Joshua that as long as he kept the Torah, "As I was with Moses, so shall I be with you" (Joshua 1:5 and 3:7).

Joshua 9

"To This Very Day"

In this chapter, we meet the inhabitants of Gibeon, a place not too distant from present-day Jerusalem, whose inhabitants hoodwinked the Israelites into coming to peaceful terms with them. By falsely giving the appearance of distant travelers (such as by carrying moldy bread, 12), they got Joshua and the elders to make a covenant with them. When the Israelites discovered the truth, however, they did not renege on their agreement granting them protection from any harm (19). Rather, they came up with the stratagem of declaring them to be "hewers of wood and drawers of water" (21)—permanent public servants—which they remained "to this very day" (29).

The obvious question (which, to be honest, we might have raised already apropos of 4:9, 5:9, 6:25, 7:26, and 8:28–29) is, to which "very day" (*ha-yom ha-zeh*) is the verse referring? Don Isaac Abravanel (1437–1508) devoted an extensive analysis to this question, arriving, in the process, at a highly unorthodox conclusion. Citing these and other examples in the introduction to his commentary on the Book of Joshua, he dismissed the talmudic implication that the words were written by Joshua himself because such notice is pointless when the narration follows so closely upon the events themselves. Rather, he maintained that the Book of Joshua, along with the Book of Judges and the Book of Samuel, were all written later (by which he could have meant "edited") by the Prophet Samuel, which would put an appreciable amount of time between the actual occurrences and the telltale "to this very day."

Joshua 10

Did the Sun Really Stand Still?

While the precise circumstances of our chapter are relatively unknown, some of its lines are quite famous, particularly, "Sun stand still in Gibeon and moon in the valley of Ayalon" (12).

Although popular lore tends to take this literally—and even searches ancient records for evidence of related astronomical phenomena—some Jewish authorities found that interpretation untenable. Here, for instance is the commentary of Gersonides (R. Levi ben Gershom, known as Ralbag; Provence, 1288–1344):

> One of the many worthy questions raised by this episode is that if the sun stood still and its visible movement was

nullified, then this wonder would be greater by far than all the wonders performed by Moses. All of those concerned natural phenomena of a lower order, while this is of a significantly higher order.... If this were so, it would contradict the Torah's stipulation that "No prophet comparable to Moses has arisen for Israel... in respect of all the wonders and signs that he performed in sight of all Israel" (Deut. 34:10–11).

How, then, does Gersonides interpret the verse? He considers it a figure of speech, comparable to "time stood still." Just as we might use that expression to describe an activity that took less time than anticipated, so does the Book of Joshua. Saying that "the sun stood still," signifies that the pursuit and subduing of the combined enemy forces gathered at Gibeon that ordinarily would have taken more time than was available at that hour of the day (since battles were not fought at night), was, miraculously, accomplished in a limited amount of daylight.

Joshua 11

All the King's Horses...

In this chapter, the Israelites must overcome a broad coalition of Canaanite forces arrayed against them at a place called Mei Merom. While some of their places of origin are unidentified (Madon, Shimron, Akhshaf), they are led by the king of Hatzor in the Upper Galilee, today a UNESCO World Heritage site, whose excavation by Yigal Yadin was a milestone in Israeli biblical archaeology. At the time of Joshua, Hatzor was something akin to a regional center ("the head [*rosh*] of all those other kingdoms" v. 11), so it is understandable why the king of Hatzor would play a central role in this affair.

God told Joshua "not to fear," promised him victory over this vast enemy, and instructed him "to hamstring their horses and burn their chariots" (6). Since the battle would already have been won, what point could there be in doing permanent damage to the horses?

In our comments on Chapter Six, we addressed the weaning of the Israelites off their dependence on divine intervention and their training to gradually assume responsibility for their own destiny. This act, for all that it appears to be gratuitous cruelty to animals, is another step in that process. Horses served military functions almost exclusively— throughout the Bible, oxen pull the plows, donkeys are the beasts of burden, and long trips are taken on camels—so God ordered them to destroy the enemy's chariots and hamstring their horses to reinforce the point that the Israelites' fortunes of war depended not only on their growing military prowess but on their obedience to Him, as well.

As the Psalmist put it: "These may [depend on] chariots and those may [depend on] horses, but we will [put our trust in] calling on the Lord our God" (20:8).

Joshua 12

What's in a Name?

From here through chapter 19, the Book of Joshua contains a vast assortment of place names. This presents an opportunity to introduce the subject of "onomastics," as the study of proper nouns is called. In each such chapter, we will select one place name and elaborate on it. To assist us, we shall consult one of the published works of Yoel Elitzur, an Israeli Bible scholar who specializes in this area.

This chapter contains the names of thirty-one places whose kings were defeated by Joshua and which were going to be distributed among the Israelites as their ancestral inheritance. However, before listing their names, the book takes a retrospective glance at a slightly earlier era, recalling the Israelite victory over Sihon, King of Cheshbon (2). Let us see how the name and location of Cheshbon were preserved.

First of all, we need to take note of the fact that a book called *Onomasticon* was written in the early 4th century CE by Eusebius, a Christian Bible scholar, who had the advantage of living in the Land of Israel (Caesarea). Calling that city by the Greek name *Essebon* (classical authors had trouble pronouncing guttural consonants like *chet*), he located it in the mountains about 20 miles east of Jericho. Moving to the mid-7th century, we should also acknowledge the contribution of the conquering Muslims, who kept most of the biblical place names, albeit giving them an Arabic flavor. Cheshbon became *Chisban* and is situated about 20 kilometers southwest of Amman. It is called by that very name by Eshtor HaParchi, the first Jewish traveler (14th century) to record biblical onomastics in his book *Kaftor Va-Ferach*.

It remains anyone's guess (do you have one?) whether the name is connected to the idea of thinking or reckoning, both of which, in Hebrew, use the root CH-SH-B.

Joshua 13

The "Leftover" Land

Occasionally, people or nations arrive at an unanticipated moment and are forced to confront an unforeseen circumstance. Such a moment was reached in this chapter: "This is the leftover land, all the regions of the Philistines and the Geshurites" (2). Up to this point, we assumed that the conquest of the entire Land of Israel was inevitable. In the immediately previous chapter, we noted the names of no fewer than thirty-one local chieftains whose locales were conquered by Joshua; now, suddenly, we discover that there are sizeable tracts of land that resisted takeover. The entire coastal plain from the Sinai Peninsula

("Teiman") north to Lebanon ("Sidon"), the Anti-Lebanon Mountains (that form the present-day border between Syria and Lebanon) up to Mount Hermon, and what appear to be parts of the Galilee, all remained in the hands of the Philistines, Geshurites, and Canaanites.

In other words, significant parcels of land held out against the Israelites. The Geshurites "continued to live among the Israelites down to this very day" (13; cf. our comments on "this very day" in chapter 9), and the Philistines would remain a thorn in their side throughout the era of the Judges (Samson) and the early monarchy (Saul). Indeed, the reference to a thorn reminds us that the Torah had foretold this, warning: "If you fail to remove the inhabitants of the land before you, those who remain will become thorns in your eyes and spikes in your sides" (Numbers 33:55). Conceivably, the reason for this setback could be related to the Israelites' lack of strict obedience to God's rules of warfare, as exemplified by the incident of the spoils of Jericho (discussed in Chapter 7).

The immediate problem, though, concerned apportioning the land amongst the nine and one-half tribes (7) who had received no distribution east of the Jordan (8ff.). Was Joshua to limit its dispersal to the territory he actually controlled? Could he, realistically, distribute land that remained unconquered? God gave him an unambiguous answer: "I will evict them before Israel; go ahead and make it part of the land-lottery as I instructed you" (6). It appears, once again, that we have arrived at a conjunction of national effort and reliance on divine intercession (see our comments on chapters 6 and 11).

Joshua 14

Caleb, Hebron, and Al-Khalil

In Chapter 12, we introduced the subject of "onomastica," the study of proper nouns, which we illustrated via the Amorite city of Cheshbon. The names that will concern us in this chapter are those of Caleb, erstwhile scout, and the city of Hebron, which was vouchsafed to him by Moses in reward for his steadfastness (Numbers 14:24).

Caleb (Hebrew: K-L-B) is clearly related to the noun *kelev*, "dog," an association that we might find less outlandish if we recall that many contemporary names have animal origins as well. For instance, Zoe (from the same Greek root that gives us zoo) is the equivalent of *Hava/Haya* (animal) and, in Hebrew, *Ze'ev* is a wolf, *Dov* is a bear, *Devorah* is a bee, and *Zvi* is a deer. Perhaps coincidentally, the most striking conglomeration of animal names in the Bible occurs among the names of the scouts Caleb accompanied (Numbers 13), including Gadi and Gadiel (kid), Susi (horse), and Gemali (camel). (If we stretch beyond Hebrew into Aramaic, we could add one more to that company: Nun, father of Joshua, means "fish").

Hebron, from the Hebrew root CH-B-R, implies attachment or friendship (which is a social attachment), and its origin probably lies in the social relationship of its four original inhabitants, on account of which it was first called Kiryat Arba (14, and 15:13–14). However, unlike Heshbon (a name Hebron also resembles linguistically), which was just given an Arabic sound (*Hisban*) by the Muslim conquerors, Hebron was translated into Arabic *Khalil*, which means a companion. (There are sources in which its name is given, more specifically, as *Khalil Al-Rahman*, The Companion of the Compassionate, i.e., God.)

Here, we have an example of how a Muslim practice perpetuated a Jewish tradition. According to a Midrash (*Bereishit Rabbah* 84:14), Hebron was so called because Abraham was regarded as a companion of God (*chaver na'eh*). Since he was already regarded as an ancestor of the Arabs and is recognized in the Qur'an as a true prophet, they decided to honor him by calling his city after his pseudonym. Likewise, the Arabic name for the western gate of the Old City of Jerusalem—*Sha'ar Yaffo* in Hebrew—is *Bab al-Khalil*, Hebron gate.

Joshua 15

A Really Tall Tale

In our explanation of the origins and development of the name Hebron (chapter 14), we noted that it had also been called Kiryat Arba on account of four of its previous inhabitants. In this chapter, we are provided with the additional information that three of those inhabitants, who were displaced by Caleb, were *'anaqim*, named Ahiman, Sheshay, and Talmay (14). Are *'anaqim*, "giants," as almost universally presumed, and can we ascertain what that meant objectively?

If I ask you to name a giant in the Bible, you would almost certainly answer Goliath, whose extraordinary height the Bible reports as "six cubits and a hand span" (1 Samuel 17:3). Considering (a) according to the *Guinness Book* of records, "the tallest man in medical history for whom there is irrefutable evidence" stood 8 ft. 11.1 inches tall, and (b) that a cubit is estimated between 1½ and 2 feet, a nine-foot-tall Goliath is incredible, but not outside the realm of empirical possibility. The more curious fact, for our investigation, is that Tanakh does not specifically call Goliath *'anaq*.

Note that all 18 usages of *'anaq* occur in either Numbers, Deuteronomy, Joshua, or Judges (8 of them in Joshua alone), indicating that its use is confined to the particular era those books encompass, namely the conquest of the Land of Israel. Deriving from a poetic Hebrew word for "neck," *'anaqim* may be defined as "long-necked ones," although an alternate derivation would designate them as descendants of someone named 'Anaq, who was their father or ancestor (13–14).

Earlier in the conquest (Joshua 11), it was reported that Joshua eliminated the *'anaqim* from Hebron and the Judean hills (21) and that they remained only in Gaza, Gat, and Ashkelon (v. 22), three cities of the Philistines. Arguably, Tanakh expects us to span the gap ourselves. If Goliath was an exceptionally tall man from Gat, he was, implicitly, an *'anaq*, so perhaps there was no need to stipulate it in the text.

Joshua 16

Just How Many Bethel's Are There?

The opening verse of this chapter names Beit-El as one the boundaries of the tribes of Joseph (i.e., Ephraim and half of Manasseh). We have made an earlier acquaintance with a place by that very symbolic name. Is it one and the same?

Abraham, shortly after his initial arrival in the land, "removed [his camp] from there to the mountains east of Bethel where he pitched his tent. Bethel was to his west and the Ai was to his east; there he built an altar to the Lord and proclaimed the Lord's name" (Genesis 12:8). Later, on his return from Egypt, "He continued on his way from the south towards Bethel where his tent had been previously, between Bethel and the Ai. To the site of the altar he erected previously…" (13:3–4).

Jacob, arising in the morning following his remarkable dream, declared that site to be awesome (*nora'*) and exclaimed: "This is none other than the house of God (*beit Elohim*); the gateway to heaven" (28:17), on account of which he subsequently changed its name from Luz to Bethel (19). Since Jacob's Bethel had been Luz heretofore, it would be reasonable to assume that it was someplace other than Abraham's Bethel, which would have been so-called even at the time of Jacob.

On the other hand, it is also reasonable to assume that if Jacob knew that there was a site at which his grandfather had "proclaimed the Lord's name," it would have been a natural place for him to have spent the night. Indeed, the Aggadah (quoted by Rashi, Genesis 28:17), has Jacob, having bypassed the site on his way from Beersheba to Haran, say, rhetorically, "Could I have passed by a place where my ancestors prayed and not have paused to pray there myself?"

There is another Bethel in the biblical future. When the Davidic kingdom split in two, the usurper, Jeroboam ben Nebat—determined to prevent continued pilgrimage to Jerusalem—erected a golden calf in Bethel, and made it a cultic center (1 Kings 12:29ff.). Since Jeroboam was from the tribe of Ephraim, it stands to reason that he would choose a "hometown" that would continue to compete with the Temple until the eventual termination of the northern kingdom he founded.

The current Israeli settlement of Bethel (Beit El), some 10 miles (17 kilometers) north of Jerusalem, appears to be situated on or near the biblical site, as the Arabic name (Beitin) of a nearby village also testifies.

Joshua 17

A Long-Lasting Legacy

Toward the end of the Book of Numbers, Moses (along with Elazar the Priest and the tribal princes) was confronted by the five orphaned daughters of Zelophehad, who demanded their fair share of the territory that was allocated to their late father. Moses submitted their case before God, Who found in their favor—providing for the distribution of inheritance to daughters in the absence of sons (Numbers 27:1ff.). At the book's very end (which happens to coincide with the end of the forty years' wandering in the wilderness), the incident is reprised with the additional information that they married cousins (37:11) thereby keeping their inheritance all in the family, so to speak, which meant the tribe of Manasseh.

This incident was a defining moment in Torah law as a rare decision in a matter we would call "women's rights." Suffice it to say in this context that the Sages did not regard these women as protestors and social activists, describing them instead as "wise, lawyerly, and virtuous" (*hakhamot, darshaniyot, tzidkaniyot*; *Bava Batra* 119b).

In the current chapter, the case reaches its fruition as the women approached Joshua (along with Elazar the Priest and the tribal princes) and the earlier divine verdict was implemented in practice: "And he gave them inheritance among their uncles" (4). Interestingly, while this ends the biblical story of Zelophehad's daughters, it has an extra-biblical epilogue.

A place named Tirzah (after one of the daughters?) is mentioned in Tanakh as the first capital of the northern kingdom, which, presumably, would locate it in the proximity of the later capital, Samaria (Shomron). In 1910, the archaeologist Gerhard Reisner found some sixty inscribed potsherds that have come to be known as "The Samaria Ostraca." Dated to the end of the 8th century BCE (around the time of King Ahab of Israel), they served as commercial records. Thirty of them contain names of nearby clans or districts of the tribe of Manasseh, including one place named Haglah and another named No'ah—evidently after another two of Zelophehad's daughters.

28 centuries—what longer-lasting legacy could these women have bequeathed?

Joshua 18

An Orientation

Before we get further into more of the minute details of how the land was apportioned among the remaining tribes, we would do well to consider some of the larger aspects.

Each tribe's portion is described in terms of its boundaries, which are noted according to each of the four cardinal directions. The Hebrew term for boundary is *gevul*; *tzafon* is north, *negev* is south, *yam* is west, and *kedem* is east. What are the etymologies of these words?

The noun *gevul* derives from a verb that means "to demarcate." We encountered it, first, on the eve of the revelation at Sinai when God instructed Moses to "demarcate (*hagbel*) the mountain and sanctify it" (Exodus 19:23), and, again, in the prohibition "Do not displace the demarcations (*gevul*) delineated (*gav'lu*) by your predecessors" (Deut. 19:14). Rather than lines on a map, these demarcations were most likely boundary stones; indeed, in Arabic, a Semitic language closely related to Hebrew, *g-b-l* means "mountain," the earliest and most natural form of boundary. (The island of Gibraltar was originally named *G-B-L Tarik* after the Arab conqueror of Spain, Tarik Ibn Ziyad.)

Yam (12) is "west" in biblical geography because the Mediterranean Sea lies to Israel's west, whereas *negev* (13) is south because the verb N-G-B means to dry, and the driest part of Israel lies to its south. *Tzafon* (5) is a bit of a puzzle because its only meaning in Hebrew is "hidden," which may be a way of signifying that in the east-west arc of the "Fertile Crescent" (Mesopotamia-Egypt), anything off to the north was out of the way. (Curiously, in Arabic, "south" is *g-n-b*, Hebrew for "stolen, or hidden away.")

Mizrach (7), for "east," is the place of shining (of the sun), just as its correspondent, *Ma'arav*, "west" (absent in our chapter), is the place of its setting.

Nevertheless, it is the term *kedem* (20) that is the most intriguing. Its other meanings in Hebrew include "front" and "before," indicating that it is the direction right in front of me. Since I can face any direction, however, there needs to be a more objective sense to it. Since the cardinal direction I can count on finding under almost any circumstance is east—as long as I await sunrise—there is an implicit assumption that we start by facing eastward. That is why even in English we call directional alignment "orientation," because it is anchored in the east, the direction of the rising sun.

Joshua 19

"Where in the World Is… Dan?"

According to our chapter (beginning in v. 40), the allotment of the tribe of Dan was situated near the center of the Land of Israel. Indeed some of the places named therein continue to resonate today, including Tzar'ah and Eshta'ol (which we will reencounter in the saga of Samson) and 'Ir Shemesh (probably Beit Shemesh), which are well-known sites in the "corridor" leading from Jerusalem westward to the coastal plain.

For that matter, so is Sha'albin (42), today a kibbutz and yeshivah not far from Ben Gurion Airport. Yehud and B'nai B'raq (45) are exits on Israel's north-south Route 4, and even Gat Rimon (same verse) could be construed as an anagram of nearby Ramat Gan. The Yarkon River and Jaffa are mentioned as well (46), and while we would not expect a reference to Tel Aviv (which was built only in 1909!), vestiges of the Dan settlement survive in the name of the region in which Tel Aviv is situated (Gush Dan) and the fact that the bus cooperative that serves Israel's largest city is likewise named Dan.

The chapter, however, also includes an account of how Dan conquered a northern site named Leshem, slew its inhabitants, and renamed it Dan after their eponymous ancestor (47). Curiously, an identical account, occurring after the death of Joshua, is narrated in Judges 18:27ff (save for the substitution of Layish for Leshem, a change that can be accounted for in Hebrew philology). If the tribe of Dan waged but a single campaign of conquest, why are there two iterations, and if its conquest of Leshem was not part and parcel of its divinely ordained allocation, how was it justified? Medieval exegetes addressed both issues.

Rashi wrote that "At this point, they took only a small portion, but the lot also fell for them in another place which was distant from their boundary." It was only after the other tribes completed the conquest of the intervening territory that Dan was able to move northward and conclude its own settlement. Rashi's disciple Yosef Kara took a slightly different tack, arguing that their initial settlement was insufficient for their needs, so they sought to expand their territory, choosing Leshem because of its name, meaning "jacinth," which was the stone on the high-priest's breastplate on which the name of their tribe was inscribed (Exodus 28:19).

Either way, this is why the most northern nature reserve in Israel is called Tel Dan.

Joshua 20

Refuge & Rehabilitation

God instructed Moses to allocate six Levitical cities as cities of refuge (Numbers 35). Moses set aside three such cities in Trans-Jordan (Deut. 4 and 19), leaving the balance to be determined later. Now, with the conquest and apportionment nearing their conclusion,

Joshua completed the assignment by allocating three additional cities of refuge west of the Jordan. Detailed principles of asylum were developed in talmudic tractate *Makkot* (Chapter Two) and canonized by Maimonides in his *Mishneh Torah*. I should like to cite one singular aspect of those laws here.

Our chapter prescribes that the unpremeditated killer "shall reside (*yashav*) in that city until he stands trial" (6, cf. Numbers 35:25). Elsewhere, the Torah qualifies that residence as "that he might live" (*vahay*; Deut. 4:42, 19:5) One of the points taken up in the Maimonidean exposition pertains to the nature of that dwelling and living.

> If a disciple [of the Sages] is exiled to a city of refuge, his teacher is exiled, too. To wit: "that he might live," enable him to live; and the lives of scholars bereft of wisdom is akin to death. Likewise, if a teacher is exiled, so is his academy (*Laws of Murder and the Preservation of Life* 7:1).

Imagine an entire academy forced to reside in a city of refuge because their master killed someone without premeditation! None of them shares his guilt; indeed, even he, strictly speaking, is not guilty; yet they are all obliged to seek asylum in order that their collective Torah learning should not be compromised.

One would be entitled to conclude from this, and similar laws, that Maimonides would support the position taken by many contemporary penologists that the principal purpose of incarceration is to provide opportunities for rehabilitation—spiritual and psychological, too—as it is implied in the name of the agency that oversees prisons: The Department of Corrections.

Joshua 21

Levitical and Aaronic Cities

In the previous chapter, we noted that the six cities of refuge were "Levitical cities." In the present chapter, we discover that there were, all told, 48 such cities. Since the tribe of Levi received no allocation of its own ("the Lord is his allocation," Deut. 10:9, 18:2), each of the other tribes ceded some its own cities to Levi.

The detailed parceling out of these cities indicates that the guiding principle of their distribution—as noted here by Rashi—was "Take more from a larger [portion] and less from a smaller [portion], each according to his inheritance shall give of his cities to the Levi'im" (Numbers 35:8). So the tribes of Judah, Simeon, and Benjamin gave 13 (4); Ephraim, Dan, and half of Manasseh gave 10 (5); Issachar, Asher, Naftali, and the other half of Manasseh gave 13 (6); and Reuben, Gad, and Zebulun gave 12 (7).

On the Levitical end, the clan of Kehat received 10 cities (v.26), Gershon 13 cities (33), and Merari 12 cities (38). But that adds up to only 35 cities, leaving a balance of 13. The resolution to our conundrum comes as a surprise: 13 cities were allocated directly to another clan of Levites, the sons of Aaron (19).

One of these cities, Anatot (18), was to become the home of the Prophet Jeremiah (Jer. 1:1). Another, Gibeon (17), reminds us that its indigenous inhabitants were assigned to everlasting service in "the House of the Lord" (Joshua 9:23). Curiously, Nob—the only city to be explicitly called a "priestly city" (1 Samuel 22:19; according to Rabbinic tradition, Nob housed the Tabernacle for 13 years)—is not listed in our chapter, leading to speculation that it was not an independent city but an adjunct of Anatot (cf. Isaiah 11: 30–32 and Nehemiah 11:32).

By talmudic law (*Makkot* 10a), priestly cities, as well as Levitical cities, also served as de facto cities of refuge, maximizing the opportunities for unpremeditated killers to escape the anticipated blood vengeance of the victim's relatives and minimizing the potential miscarriages of justice.

Joshua 22

The First Exercise in Israel-Diaspora Relations

Just as the allocation of the land amongst the tribes and the establishment of the cities of refuge fulfilled conditions laid down by Moses, so does the current chapter satisfy the terms he set out for the tribes of Reuben, Gad, and half of Manasseh: "If you volunteer for military service… and serve until the Lord disperses His enemies… and the land is conquered… then you will be entitled to your land" (Numbers 32:20ff.).

After 14 years of conquest, Joshua permitted these two and one half tribes to return to their families and possessions on the eastern bank of the Jordan. Prior to crossing, however, they paused to erect an imposing altar (10), triggering the suspicions of the remaining tribes that the purpose of the altar was idolatrous. A delegation led by the High Priest Phinehas (14) determined that their intentions were pure, and the potential for a civil war was defused.

The argument the tribes of Trans-Jordan offered in their defense resonates with a contemporary issue: the relationship between the Jews of Israel and Diaspora Jewry. Here is what the departing tribes said to their brothers remaining in Israel:

> We have acted out of anxiety lest your children challenge our children in the future saying, What have you to do with

the Lord God of Israel? God made the Jordan the boundary between us… You have no share in the Lord… So we have erected this altar… to serve as an everlasting witness between us… (21–29)

Even though they had fought side by side for 14 years and the physical distance that was to divide them was minimal, there was still the fear that their separation would lead to their spiritual and religious estrangement.

How much more so should we worry about the prospects of the alienation of Diaspora Jewry from Israel, given the considerable increase of both time and distance, and work toward sustaining mutual understanding and support?

Joshua 23

Assimilation: A Very "Thorny" Subject

Joshua was particularly anxious about the prospective dangers of assimilation and intermarriage, and he warned the people not to tolerate the presence of idolaters in their midst lest they pose an existential threat to God's nation.

> Know for certain that the Lord your God will not continue to drive these nations out before you; they shall become a snare and a trap for you, a scourge to your sides and thorns (*tzeninim*) in your eyes, until you perish from this good land that the Lord your God has given you (13).

Both the thought and its literary formulation are familiar to us from an identical warning that Moses issued to the people shortly before his own departure.

> But if you do not dispossess the inhabitants of the land, those whom you allow to remain shall be stings (*tzeninim*) in your eyes and thorns in your sides, and they shall harass you in the land in which you live (Num. 33:55).

These are the only two places in the entire Tanakh in which the word *tzeninim* appears, and the word's use in identical contexts strongly supports the assumption that Joshua was deliberately paraphrasing a Torah verse. While this observation alone is hardly novel or unexpected, in a retrospective we will soon offer on the Book of Joshua, we will explain why Joshua consistently displayed a preference for the Book of Numbers—as he did in this instance.

Joshua 24

Why Feature Balaam?

In this final chapter, we read Joshua's valedictory. It takes the form of a concise retrospective on Jewish history from its dawning in the age of the patriarchs (2–4) through the slavery in, and exodus from, Egypt (5–7), crossing the wilderness (7–9), and the conquest of Canaan (11–13).

One detail from each successive era is included: God's distinction between Jacob and Esau; the crossing of the Red Sea; Balaam's unsuccessful attempt to curse Israel; and the conquest of Jericho. Arguably, of all that transpired during the forty years in the wilderness, the episode involving Balaam is hardly the most noteworthy; why was it alone chosen?

I would suggest that the answer lies in the singularity of the threat

Balaam posed to the Jewish nation and the unique way in which that threat was neutralized. Most of the threats that confronted them from the exodus on, were either military or intramural. By this point in time, they had ample opportunity to savor their own military prowess—as demonstrated by their successful conquests—and their defusing of the potential conflict with the tribes of Trans-Jordan (Chapter 22) dispelled the internal threat as well.

That left a threat of a theological variety, and Balaam met this specification. His was not the threat of open warfare, but of virulent anti-Semitism, and his assumption that Israel stood in divine disfavor was countered only by a remarkable display of divine favor: "I refused to listen to Balaam and he blessed you exceedingly and I rescued you from him" (10).

Retrospective

Joshua Preserves and Adapts Tradition

As I approached the end of the Book of Joshua, I thought to compare his valedictory with that of Moses.

In chapter 23, I observed that there are only two places in the entire Tanakh in which the word *tzeninim* appears, and its use in identical contexts strongly supports the assumption that Joshua was deliberately paraphrasing a Torah verse. This observation alone is hardly novel or unexpected; however, it joined with several earlier observations (noted in previous chapters) to invite the following conclusion: That book of the Torah that is reprised most often in Joshua is the Book of Numbers. Here are the instances:

- Dispatching spies to Jericho (Chapter 2) reprises Moses' sending spies (Numbers 12).
- The laws of spoils, evoked apropos of the conquest of Jericho (7), were introduced after the battle against Midian (Numbers 31).
- The right of the daughters of Zelophehad to inherit (17) was anticipated in Numbers 27.
- The establishment of cities of refuge (20) completes an endeavor begun by Moses (Numbers 35).
- Allocating Levitical cities (21) was founded on a principle expounded in Numbers 35.
- Joshua (22) concluded the deal that Moses struck with Reuben Gad and half- Manasseh (Numbers 32).
- The dire consequences of tolerating the prolonged presence of idolaters (23) was anticipated in Numbers 33.
- The sole specific incident recalled of the forty years in the

wilderness (24) is Balaam's frustrated attempt to curse Israel (Numbers 22ff.).

Why so? Because the Book of Joshua picks up chronologically where Numbers ends—at the juncture of Moses's death. The entire Book of Deuteronomy takes up but one week: It commences on the first of Adar (Deut. 1:3: "In the fortieth year, on the first day of the twelfth month") and concludes with Moses's death on the seventh of that very month (according to Rabbinic tradition). But perhaps of greater import is the lesson this teaches us about leadership. When a leader dies, the Torah principles that person established do not likewise expire. The successor is charged with the responsibility of maintaining tradition, yet the gifted leader must, within Torah parameters, adapt that tradition to new times and generations.

Judges

Gustave Doré, *Deborah Praises Jael* (1866)

Judges 1

Transitions

The Book of Judges opens just like the Book of Joshua did: with the death of a beloved long-time leader and the nation facing the prospect of moving forward bereft of inspired and inspirational guidance.

Unlike the previous instance, however, this time there is no leader-in-waiting. Moses had groomed Joshua to succeed him (although his appointment also required divine approval), but Joshua had not done the same. Joshua was first succeeded by anonymous elders "who were acquainted with all the deeds God had performed for Israel" (Joshua 24:31)—arguably, a reference to members of the generation that had reached the age of twenty after the failed mission of the scouts (see Numbers 14:29ff.)—and there is an allusion to the continuation of the "old guard" in the reference to Eliezer, son of Aaron, the High Priest (Joshua 24:33), but no single individual came forward to assume command.

Hence, God appointed a collective leadership: the tribe of Judah (2), which was reluctant to operate independently and, instead, called on its brother tribe of Simeon to share the leadership role (3). Curiously, while the chapter goes on to detail Judah's military successes as well as those of the tribes of Ephraim and Manasseh, it makes but passing reference to Simeon's conquest of Safed, after which that tribe essentially disappears from the balance of biblical history.

Given the collective nature of the leadership post-Joshua, it is somewhat incongruous that the Book of Judges, as its very name implies, features lone leaders. Indeed, as we move to chapter 2, we will witness a reprise of this transition with a decidedly individualistic complexion.

Judges 2

Transitions Take II: Here Come the Judges!

In the previous chapter, we observed that Joshua was not followed by a handpicked successor but by a collective leadership with the tribe of Judah at its head. In Chapter Two, Joshua's death is reported again, as is his succession by "the elders who outlived him" (7, cf. Joshua 24:31), but there is no reference to coalitions of tribes and their successful conquests. Rather, there is a segue into the tragedy of idolatry, and we revert, again, to the rule of individual leaders—called *shof'tim* (singular: *shofet*).

Customarily translated as "judges," the root Sh-F-T (recognizable in such words as *mishpat*, "justice") is closely related to the root Sh-B-T, which yields the word *shevet*—meaning both "tribe" and "staff." A *shofet*, then, is someone who wields a staff, a visible and tangible sign of power. This linguistic insight explains why the *shof'tim* of the Book of Judges are invariably military leaders and in only a single case does one of them overtly exercise judicial functions—and that, paradoxically, is the sole woman judge, Deborah (Judges 4:5, see our comments there).

Our chapter's introduction to these *shof'tim* also illustrates an axiom of the philosophy of biblical history: The fate of the Jewish nation is inextricably linked to its obedience to God. Resolute Torah observance advances its fortunes, noncompliance leads to breakdown, and idolatry—the quintessence of disaffection—invites devastation.

In the words of the text: God would appoint a *shofet* (16), under whose reign the Israelites would successfully resist the oppression of their enemies that was brought upon them on account of their infidelities (18), yet upon whose death they would revert to their evil ways (19). Indeed, the recalcitrance they regularly exhibited so highlighted the fickleness of their attachment to God that He delayed the completion of their conquest of the indigenous population in order to put Israel's faith to the test—precisely as Joshua had anticipated (Chapter 23).

That they ignored his caution is lamentable; that they did so repeatedly—inviting the cycles of oppression and redemption—is an enduring conundrum that even the subsequent millennia of Jewish history have failed to resolve.

Judges 3

On the Ups and Downs of Right and Left

In Romance languages as well as in English, right-handedness is positive, and left-handedness is negative. In French, "right" is *droit* (English: adroit), while "left" is *gauche* (clumsy). In Italian, "right" is *destra* (English: dexterous), while "left" is *sinistra* (sinister). In this chapter, we encounter Ehud ben Gera, a conspicuously left-handed *shofet*, who assassinated Eglon the King of Moab.

Ehud is introduced as *ben ha-yemini* (15), which in Hebrew is either—literally—a "son of the right [hand]" (=under the sway of the right hand, on the analogy of a *bar mitzvah*=under the sway of mitzvah obligation) or another way of saying that he was of the tribe of Benjamin. He is further described as *ish iter yad yemino* (same verse), which is traditionally understood to mean his right arm was withered or shrunken. This expression makes only one other appearance in the whole Tanakh, in Judges 20:16, where it is applied to 700 exceptional soldiers from the tribe of Benjamin. Finally, he girded his dagger about his waist on the right side (16) and drew it out with his left hand to stab Eglon (21).

Our analysis is somewhat perplexing. We have someone who is

called a *yemini** because he came from the tribe of Benjamin, but who used his left hand because his right hand was unserviceable. Indeed, his tribe's name, suggesting right-handedness, is belied by the fact that—at one point—it appears to have spawned a whole clan of accomplished left-handed warriors, as noted above.

Of course, an alternative possibility is that Ehud, like most people, was right-handed. However, in order to evade discovery of his dagger when he entered Eglon's chamber, he buckled it on his right-hand side where it would not be detected. But that meant he would have to draw it with his left hand, so he trained himself to be ambidextrous (*iter?*). This may have set a precedent for his fellow Benjaminites, who then made ambidexterity a tribal virtue.

*If the word *yemini* looks like Yemenite, it is because *yamin* is Arabic for south and Yemen is the southernmost country on the Arabian Peninsula. (See our comments to Joshua 18 on geographical orientation.)

Judges 4

Deborah, a Paradox: Prophetess, Judge, and General

Deborah was paradoxical in several respects. In a strictly patriarchal world, she was a prophetess (*nevi'ah*), a judge (*shof'tah*), and, like the other *shof'tim* (see our comments on Chapter Two), a military leader. Such exceptionalism invites explanation, and several rabbinic and medieval sources attempt to provide it.

The Talmud names Deborah among the seven Israelite prophetesses (*Megillah* 14a), and a Midrash attributes both her prophetic and judicial status to her simultaneous devotion to her husband and to God, demonstrated by her encouraging him to advance his social standing by manufacturing wicks (hence, *Lapidot* v.4) for the lamps in the Tabernacle at Shiloh (*Tanna d'Bei Eliyahu* 10). Rabbi Yehudah Halevi—as per his philosophical views—would argue that God can bestow the capacity for prophecy on anyone, women included, while Maimonides would submit that prophecy is a perfection of the intellective and imaginative faculties, of which women, too, are capable. Abravanel added the observation that anyone who could meet the Maimonidean requirements for prophecy would most assuredly command respect and that accounts for her acceptance as a judge, as well.

Another tradition, embodied in an expansive Aramaic translation (*targum*), attributes to her great wealth, interpreting her "palm tree" (*tomer*, 4) as "She owned palms in Jericho, orchards in Ramah, olives in Beit El, and productive soil in Tur Malka." A later Midrash takes the "palm tree" more literally, justifying her service as a judge—considering the restriction on male-female interactions—by identifying it as a public place where she conducted her court (*Yalkut Shim'oni* 42). The Zohar amplifies her accomplishments to such an extent that it declares: "Two women, of the entire world, recited the praises of the Holy One, blessed be He, as no men in the world were ever capable" (3:19). They are Deborah and Hannah (of whom we shall learn more when we reach 1 Samuel).

However, an alternative school of thought considers the title *nevi'ah* to mean a prophet's wife, identifying Deborah as the wife of Barak ben Avinoam (*barak*, "lightning," being related, semantically, to *lapidot*, "torches"), and attributes the manufacture of wicks to her; all considerably more traditionally feminine roles than those delineated above.

IN THE COMPANY OF PROPHETS

Judges 5

What Does Sinai Have to Do with Sisera?

The "Song of Deborah" belongs to a tradition that extends back to the crossing of the Red Sea of celebrating military victory in song. Indeed, this chapter is part of the *haftarah* (additional Prophetic reading) that accompanies the weekly Torah portion of *Beshallah* (Exodus 13:17ff.) that incorporates the crossing and its accompanying song. A striking distinction between the two is that the crossing of the sea, having been led by Moses, was celebrated first by him and the men (Exodus 15:1) and only later by Miriam and the women (15:20). The victory over Sisera, having been initiated by Deborah, allows her name to precede that of Barak, the male general (1).

One detail of the song is the focus of one of the most enlightening and critical disputes in medieval biblical exegesis. It pits Rashi, the embodiment of rabbinically inspired interpretation, against a younger colleague of his, Rabbi Yosef Kara, one of the earliest champions of rationally inclined analysis. The verse in question reads: "Lord, when you went forth out of Seir, when you marched out of the field of Edom, earth trembled, heavens also released, yes, the clouds released water" (4).

Rashi, basing himself on the talmudic narrative (Aggadah) that prior to offering the Torah to Israel, God had offered it to the Edomites, who had refused it, commented: "This refers to the giving of Torah." Kara countered by saying: "What place does the revelation of Torah at Sinai have here? I have reviewed all the songs recorded in Scripture about miracles that were performed for Israel and have found that they all relate to their [historical] circumstances." Moreover, according to Kara, Scripture is deemed always to be self-sufficient for its own interpretation: "Besides, it is uncustomary for a prophet in any of the 24 [canonical] books to speak so enigmatically that we would require an Aggadah to understand him."

The tension between interpretations based solely upon rabbinic tradition and those that also incorporate critical rational analysis has enriched biblical exegesis in the past and continues to do so today.

Judges 6

Who was the "Navi Man"?

In our chapter, the Israelites betray God (once again) and are delivered into the hands of the Midianites—along with assorted other desert tribes including Amalek, who raid them so incessantly and thoroughly that they are compared to the devastation caused by locusts (5). Adhering to the sequence forecast in Chapter Two (see our comments there), they cry out to God, and a savior *shofet* appears in the person of Gideon.

Let us investigate one step in this process that is detailed in v. 8: "The Lord sent a prophet-man unto the children of Israel and he said unto them, 'Thus says the Lord, the God of Israel: I brought you up from Egypt and brought you forth out of the house of bondage.'"

The commentators are unanimous in identifying this "prophet-man" (*ish navi*) with Phinehas son of Aaron, the High Priest (see Rashi, Kara, Kimhi, inter alia). On the one hand, Phinehas is named as an active leader of the people late in Joshua's career (see Joshua 22:13ff.) and there is no subsequent report of his death,* so he could, quite logically, have been the one to respond to the people here.

On the other hand, however, where was he in the interim? As Ralbag (Gersonides, 1288–1344) questioned:

One might well ask, if this prophet was present, why did he not rebuke Israel throughout his life? Why did they have to call on Deborah? To resolve this quandary, it appears that his prophecy was intermittent and was inadequate for the task of leading the people, for which reason, also, he had to appoint Gideon.

Since prophecy requires divine inspiration (see our comments to Judges 4), it was not Phinehas's choice to seize or relinquish the initiative in these matters, but God's.

* Jewish legendary tradition declared Phinehas to have defied death, even identifying him with the later prophet Elijah who, likewise, never died, as anyone knows who pours him a beaker of wine at the Passover Seder.

Judges 7

Gideon's Three Hundred

Legend has it that 300 Spartans held off a vastly larger Persian force at the Battle of Thermopylae. Gideon, too, fought with only 300 warriors, but the way he selected them is problematic.

According to our chapter, God informed Gideon that he had started out with too large an army (4) and instructed him to winnow his ranks by taking his troops to the water to drink. Most of the soldiers knelt to drink; 300 of them remained standing and lapped up the water from their cupped hands "like a dog" (5). They are the ones Gideon chose to accompany him to battle, and theirs was the victory over Midian.

The question is: Did lapping the water make them the worst soldiers or the best?

Rashi is representative of the consensus of exegetes who argue that kneeling to drink disqualified the majority because it indicated an inclination to kneel before idols. Ergo, the 300 who remained stationary were selected because of their religious superiority and, albeit outnumbered, won the battle.

Personally, I find that interpretation inadequate for two reasons. One, as the Spartans demonstrate, on any given day even just 300 elite troops can turn the tide of battle. Second, it fails to explain the depiction of their lapping "like a dog." While it may well be that this is a clinical description and carries no value judgment, I offer an alternative interpretation. The 300 men who stood and lapped like dogs were chosen because they were the least qualified and their victory enhanced Gideon's reputation as someone who was divinely sponsored and supported.

Judges 8

Gideon Declines a Throne but Creates an "Obstacle"

Gideon was a complex character. On the one hand, he displayed extraordinary humility and religious devotion. When offered a hereditary monarchy ("rule over us; you, your son, and grandson," 22), he declined, stating that "neither I nor my son shall rule over you; the Lord shall rule over you" (23).

And yet, immediately thereafter, Gideon instructed his followers to turn over the golden earrings they had taken as spoils (24), and he fashioned from them a "golden *ephod*" (apron?) "and all Israel went astray after it, and it became an obstacle to Gideon and his family" (27).

That "obstacle" (or "snare") is a euphemism for idolatry is evident in several ways. First is the solicitation of the golden earrings, which are exactly what Aaron had collected from the people to manufacture the golden calf (Exodus 32:2–3). Second is the verb used to describe Israel's attitude towards it: *va-yiznu* ("went astray"), which literally signifies harlotry or infidelity. (See our comments on Judges 1, where we defined idolatry as "the quintessence of disaffection" with God, inviting almost certain disaster.) The third indication takes us back to the Torah, which expressly refers to idolatry as "an obstacle" (Exodus 23:33) and warns the Israelites not to tolerate the presence of idolaters "lest they become an obstacle in your midst" (Exodus 34:12. See, too, our comments on Joshua 23).

Small wonder, then, that "as soon as Gideon was dead, the children of Israel again went astray after the Ba'alim" (33), they "remembered not the Lord their God, who had delivered them out of the hand of all their enemies" (34), and "they showed no kindness to the house of Jerubaal, namely Gideon" (35). These three behaviors—idolatry, infidelity, and ingratitude—were to characterize the Israelites throughout the era of the judges.

Judges 9

A Parable As Lovely As A Tree

Joyce Kilmer (who, incidentally, was killed while serving in the American army during World War I), famously wrote: "I think that I shall never see a poem as lovely as a tree." In our chapter, Yotam, youngest and sole surviving son of Gideon, disparaged his fellow Shechemites for choosing his half-brother Avimelekh to be their king. The instrument he employed was a parable about "the trees of the forest who sought themselves a king" (8ff.).

We read that the olive tree declined to rule lest it cease producing its respected oil (9), the fig tree declined lest it cease to produce its succulent fruit (11), and the vine declined lest it interrupt the production of its delightful wine (13). Finally, out of frustration, the trees turn to the lowly bramble bush, which consented to rule over them providing they can all take refuge in its meager shadow; otherwise, it threatened to ignite the entire forest (15). The moral of the parable, as Yotam related it, is that Avimelekh was unworthy of their respect. They would be unable to take refuge in his meager shadow, in which case he would ignite them, and they would be consumed by one another's flame (20).

In the continuation of the story, something akin to a civil war broke out between Avimelekh and his patrons—fulfilling Yotam's augury of a conflagration that consumed both sides. After Shechem reconciled with Avimelekh, seeing him as a lesser threat than their hired gun, Gaal ben Eved (literally, "loathsome one, son of a slave"), Avimelekh set an ambush for Gaal in the neighboring hills. As Gaal spotted the ambush, the mayor of Shechem, Zevul, reassured him that he was mistaken, claiming that "the shadow of the mountain appears to you as people" (36).

Recall that in Yotam's parable the shadow of the bramble signified Avimelekh's protection and it was meant sarcastically. How ironic that Zevul used that very figure of speech (deliberately?) to protect Avimelekh.

Judges 10

Footnotes to History?

Our chapter begins with the terse statement that someone named Tola ben Puah served as a judge over Israel for 23 years. No mention is made of which—if any—enemies he encountered, nor whether or how he prevailed; just the bare bones of his name, father's name, and his tribal affiliation (Issachar).

No greater detail is provided about the leadership role of his successor, Yair ha-Gil'adi, but there is—at least—some pertinent personal data, namely that he had thirty sons, who, together, administered thirty cities, an indication of the wealth and influence of their father.

What are we to make of these notices? Does the paucity of historical information imply their relative unimportance? On the other hand, can people who led Israel without untoward incident for twenty-three and twenty-two years, respectively, be insignificant? The Talmud stipulates that all prophecies recorded in Tanakh have enduring relevance (BT *Megillah* 14a). Our challenge is to determine the enduring value of what appears, on the surface, to be of only limited import.

Such value is provided by *Yalkut Shim'oni*, a medieval midrashic anthology, in its observation (Judges #42) that every tribe produced a judge—with the striking exception of Simeon, whose leadership potential was dealt a lethal blow by the nefarious activities of its Prince Zimri, whose dalliance with a Midianite woman is described in Numbers 25. (In our comments on Judges 1, we observed that Simeon seems to disappear from biblical history after a brief mention in the opening chapter.)

In other words, there is often significance to be found in relative insignificance. Even if neither Tola nor Yair won a striking military victory and even if their respective tenures in office were not marked by any extraordinary event, the mere fact of distributive leadership that they embody lends significance to their otherwise "ordinary" guidance. Oftentimes, even footnotes need to be read.

Judges 11

The Fate of Jephthah's Daughter

After the failure of diplomacy to settle the Israelite-Ammonite crisis (12–28), Jephthah was inspired to prepare for battle (29). In so doing, he made a vow: "If [God] will deliver the Ammonites into my hands, whatever comes out of the door of my house to greet me when I return, whole, from Ammon, will belong to the Lord; I will offer it as a sacrifice" (30–31).

The upshot is that he was greeted by his daughter, an only child (34).

While we were told three things about her; namely, "she never knew a man," "she became an ordinance (*hoq*) in Israel," and "for four days a year, Israelite maidens would lament her" (39–40), her actual fate is unclear. The Talmud and Midrash described Jephthah's vow as "inappropriate" (*shelo ke-hogen*) and maintained that he was obliged to sacrifice his daughter. They also addressed the question of why he did not simply annul his vow. Since only the high priest can annul the vow of a ruler, they posited a standoff between Jephthah and Phinehas, neither of whom would defer to the other (*Taanit* 4a; *Bereishit Rabbah* 60:3).

This view held sway until the 12th century, when an alternative interpretation was advanced. Abraham Ibn Ezra (cited by Nachmanides to Leviticus 27: 29) specified that Jephthah's vow was to be parsed as follows: "Whatsoever emerges from my doorway ... will be dedicated to God OR offered as a sacrifice" (31). Rather than sacrifice his daughter, Jephthah had her secluded and she remained a virgin her entire life. David Kimchi offered the identical parsing in the name of his father, Joseph, and it was adopted by Gersonides and Abravanel, while Nachmanides rejected it out of hand.

Judges 12

Shibboleth: Trouble with Border-Crossings

Our chapter includes a most idiosyncratic episode. During a domestic battle that left an untold number of Ephraimites dead, the survivors needed to cross the Jordan back to their own (western) bank. The Gileadites, to hamper that crossing, came up with a ruse that enabled them to distinguish between the Ephraimites, their opponents, and legitimate border crossers. They required everyone to recite the word *shibboleth*, which the Ephraimites, due to a speech defect, were unable to properly articulate. When they tried, it came out as *sibboleth*; and, with their true identities revealed, they were executed (6).

A reasonable question to pose (to an otherwise unreasonable situation) is why was *shibboleth* chosen from among all the words in Hebrew that are spelled with the letter *shin*? The answer starts with the realization that it has two meanings in Hebrew. In addition to the prevalent meaning of a "sheaf (of grain)," it is used poetically to mean a "stream (of water)." Since the Ephraimite refugees were attempting to cross a river, the use of this word is appropriate.

Another reasonable question might be, did Ephraimites alone exhibit this defect and why? Logic would imply that it was exclusive to them because otherwise it would not have been an effective criterion. As to why it affected them, Radak already speculated on that, writing: "Perhaps the climate (*avir*) of their territory caused it, just as people in France pronounce *shin* as *sav*." (In speculating about tribal peculiarities in general, recall that in Chapter Three we encountered unusually left-handed Benjaminites.)

Shibboleth was put to similar use in another historical circumstance. According to John Cleveland's 1658 account of the Watt Tyler rebellion in England, "They had a shibboleth to discover them, he who pronounced *Brot* and *Cawse* for Bread and Cheese had his head lopt off." More recently, season 2 episode 8 (2000) of the *West Wing*, in which Chinese claiming to be Christians had to validate their religious identities, was appropriately entitled "Shibboleth."

Judges 13

When Is a Mal'akh an Angel?

The Lord's angel (*mal'akh*) did not continue to appear to Manoah and his wife; that's when Manoah knew that he was the Lord's angel. Then Manoah said to his wife, 'We will surely die for we have seen a divine being (*elohim*)'" (Judges 13:21–22).

Mal'akh, usually rendered "angel," and *elohim*, usually "god," are frequently mistranslated. Some of the misunderstanding inheres in the Hebrew; the rest is due to the vicissitudes of English.

The verbal root *L-'-Kh* yields the noun *mela'khah*, meaning "labor," and a *mal'akh* is one who performs a labor (the prefix *m* here indicating agency). While logic would dictate that human labors do not need divine performers, the tendency in Bible translations and commentaries has been to treat all appearances of *mal'akh* as angels. While that would be fine in Greek, wherein *angelos* simply means "messenger," it fails in English, wherein angel has come to mean a particular messenger, i.e., one dressed in white, wearing a halo, and, usually, outfitted with a harp. In this regard, the Aramaic version of Onkelos is more discriminating, using *mal'akha* for an ethereal angel, and *izgeda* for a mortal one.

Neither has *elohim* fared better, its ubiquitous translation as "god" causing a host of theological difficulties of which *tzelem elohim* (Genesis 1:27) is just the most poignant. How can mankind be created "in the image of God" when Maimonides's second (of thirteen) articles of faith stipulates that "the blessed Creator is incorporeal"? Here, too, both Hebrew and English are deceptive. *Elohim* is a homonymous noun whose various meanings include God (Gen. 1:1), anything regarded as a deity (Exodus 20:3), a court of law (Exodus 21:6, 22:7), and nobility (Gen. 6:2, 4). However, just as the English noun "god" has an adjectival form: godly, so does *elohim* also serve as an adjective meaning divine, used as a form of hyperbole.

Ru'ah elohim (Gen. 1:2) is a ferocious wind, *mar'ot elohim* (Ezekiel 1:1) are incredible visions, and *har'rei el* (Psalms 36:7) are majestic mountains. And, to return to our original problem, *tzelem elohim* is a godly image, godly and goodly being one and the same in Olde English. In comparison with God's other creatures, the image in which he cast mankind is truly divine.

Judges 14

Samson's Riddle in *Halakhah*

Samson, known in rabbinic literature as Samson the Hero (*ha-gibbor*), was renowned for his extraordinary strength. It appears from the text of our chapter that he was quite a wit, too.

At his wedding party, Samson challenged his Philistine comrades with the following riddle, whose solution would earn them thirty linen cloaks and thirty changes of clothing: "Out of the eater came food and out of the bold came sweet" (14). Not surprisingly, they were unable to solve the riddle, because it was specific to a circumstance known only to Samson (slaying a lion and eating honey from its carcass, 6–8). Desperate to win, they coerced Samson's wife to coax the answer from him (15ff.), and he had to give them thirty changes of clothing that he took off an equal number of dead Philistines (19).

Samson's wager is cited occasionally in halakhic literature as a precedent for settling wagers that involve an element of chicanery. Here is one contemporary example, courtesy of *Hashukei Hemed*, a talmudic commentary (on *Bava Metzia* 73b) by R. Yitzchak Zylberstein of Bnei Brak (b. 1935).

Offering a prize of $100, a teacher challenged his students to count how many times Rashi, in his Talmud commentary, says "I do not know." One student came back with the correct answer, having looked it up on a computerized database. Does the teacher owe him the money?

In explaining that a specious wager does not need to be honored, Rabbi Zylberstein cited the case of Samson's riddle, pointing out that since Samson's friends resorted to a trick to answer it, he paid them only half of what he promised: thirty changes of clothing but not the thirty linen cloaks.

He ruled that, in practice, the teacher does not have to pay the money because (a) such a wager is akin to gambling and (b) the student should have understood that the teacher expected them to answer without resort to outside help.

Judges 15

Samson's Strength: A Divine Endowment

Samson's strength was unmatched. Despite being tied up with two new ropes (13), he freed himself "as though they were like flax that had been burned by fire" and did it so handily that his restraints gave the appearance of "melting" off his hands (14). That being the case, it is curious that when he was first approached by the Judeans to turn himself in to the Philistines, he administered an oath to them that "you will not attack me yourselves" (12). Why would he fear a Judean attack and not a Philistine one?

The answer to this perplexity provides an important insight into Samson's conduct, which appears to have been dependent entirely upon the immediate will of God. The key to this observation lies in the use of the verb *va-titzlach*, to come upon in a rush (root: *TZ-L-CH*), which occurs only seven times in Tanakh: twice each for Saul and David, and three times for Samson (14:6, 19; 15:14). Surely, he must have had greater than average strength to begin with, but his "superhuman" feats were always preceded by a surge of divinely inspired power.

That it was a divine endowment—rather than something that Samson could summon at will—would explain why he might fear that it would not serve him if he were to attempt to use it against the Judeans; hence, the oath not to attack him themselves. It might also explain why someone who was adjured by an angel of the Lord to be a Nazirite (13:7) could so blithely ignore the prohibition against defiling himself through contact with the corpses of the Philistines since he was divinely ordained to slay them.

Judges 16

Samson and Delilah: The Difference between Night and Day

Our chapter chronicles the denouement of the Samson saga. His infatuation with Delilah (4) was manipulated by the Philistines to expose the secret of his strength (5–6). After toying with them three times (7–9, 10–12, 13–14), he finally succumbed to her incessant nagging and revealed that he was a Nazirite, and that if his hair were cut, "My strength would leave me, I would be weakened, and likened to any other man" (17).

Delilah recognized that this time he has told her the truth ("all his heart," 18), recognition coming either because "one instinctively recognizes the truth" (Rashi) or in consequence of the fact that on the three previous occasions he admitted only to human weakness while this time he explicitly said, "my strength would leave" (Radak). After cutting his hair, the Philistines blinded him and imprisoned him at hard labor (21), and his hair gradually grew back (22). At a festival, they brought him out to make sport of him and, as is well-known, he literally brought the house down, giving his own life to take those of three thousand Philistines, "slaying more in death than he had in life" (30).

At this juncture, I would like to offer an observation based on the symbolism inherent in the names of the protagonists of this last chapter. The name *Shimshon* is derived from the Hebrew word for the sun (*shemesh*), implying purity and goodness, while if we take the "D" of *Delilah* to be a possessive prefix (which it is in Aramaic), then she was a woman of the night (*layla*), with the concomitant implications of evil and malevolence. If these were not their actual names, they were certainly well-chosen for serving as one another's nemesis.

Judges 17

Lawless Times

Our chapter raises a most grievous issue: idolatry. Micah, or Michayhu, was a man from the Ephraim hill country (1) about whom we know nothing save that his wealthy mother gave a silversmith 200 silver pieces that she had dedicated to God to fashion a graven image and a molten image (*pesel u-masekha*, 3-4). Micah set up a private sanctuary, fashioned priestly vestments (*ephod*) and paraphernalia (*t'rafim*), appointed his son as priest (5), and later hired a professional holy-man, a Levite, to augment his clergy (12), creating a kind of sacral oxymoron: a Levi-Kohen (13).

At this juncture, there are several things we need to recall. First, Ephraim has played an outsized role thus far in the book. Ehud's posse came from Ephraim (Chapter 3), Deborah lived in the Ephraim hill country (Chapter 4) as did the later judge Tola ben Puah (10), Gideon's army came from Ephraim (7–8), and Jephthah's failure to use Ephraimite soldiers led to a civil war (12). It will also help to recall that we have encountered something similar earlier in Judges apropos Gideon. In Chapter Eight, we read that Gideon instructed his followers to turn over the golden earrings they had taken as spoils (24), and he fashioned from them a "golden *ephod*" (apron?), "and all Israel went astray after it, and it became an obstacle to Gideon and his family" (27).

How could Micah, the Levite, or anyone else involved in our chapter, reconcile a private sanctuary, priestly vestments, etc., with dedication to God? Was there not an obvious—and odious—clash with the Tabernacle at Shiloh? The answer seems to arise out of verse 6 (which repeats itself in 18:1 and 21:25, the closing verse of the book): "In those days there was no king in Israel; every man did that which was right in his own eyes." According to rabbinic chronology, the events reported in the final chapters of the Book of Judges really transpired at the very beginning of that era, preceding those of Ehud, Deborah, Gideon, etc. The absence of authority—political or religious—allowed for what scholars call "syncretism," the specious combination of genuine religious devotion and superstitious practice. As to the chronological anarchy, we shall have more to say about it in the next chapter.

Judges 18

Lawless Times II

In the previous chapter, we noted that rabbinic chronology placed the episode involving Micah and his idol at the beginning of the era of the Judges, before political or religious authority had been established. As a proof text, we cited the oft-repeated verse: "In those days there was no king in Israel; every man did that which was right in his own eyes" (17:6). The present chapter opens, similarly, with: "In those days there was no king in Israel; and in those days the Danite tribe sought for themselves an inheritance to dwell in; for up to that day nothing had been allotted to them among the tribes of Israel for an inheritance."

It is from the juxtaposition of anarchy (literally, Greek for "no king") with the Danite quest for inheritance that the sages deduced the chronological sequence. As conveyed by Rashi:

> "Nothing had been allotted to them:" A suitable inheritance for them in the conquered territory, as it is said in Joshua, "The boundary of the Danites exceeded their grasp" (Joshua 19:47). This, too, teaches us that this episode took place at the very beginning of the period of the judges.

The reference to Joshua 19:47 takes us back to the time that the initial conquest of the land was still underway. In our comments to that chapter, we cited the commentaries of Rashi and R. Yosef Kara in explanation of both the sequence of events and their justification. Here, we would like to draw attention to a highly speculative observation on the nature of the conquest itself.

The text states that the five Danite scouts "came to Layish, and saw that the people there dwelt in security, after the manner of the Sidonians, quiet and secure" (7). Sidon, which is today a Lebanese port city, was one of the principal cities of the Phoenicians, the seafaring people of yore who brought their produce to the Greek islands and, along with that, elements of their culture and language. The conjunction, here, of Phoenicia, Greeks, and Israelites led some Israeli archaeologists who had explored Tel Dan in northern Israel to speculate that these Danites were not native Israelites but Aegean mercenaries (there is a Greek tribe called Danaoi) hired by the Egyptians to keep order in the region.

Judges 19

Family Reunion?

Our chapter narrates the story of a Levite living on the slopes of Mt. Ephraim whose concubine abandoned him and ran home to her parents in Bethlehem. (The verse euphemistically calls the abandonment *zenut*, harlotry, but if she had committed adultery, the husband would have been prohibited to reunite with her.) While the text provides only this information about him, we know enough at this juncture to attempt to identify him more specifically and, thereby, to link this episode to previous ones.

In Chapter 17, we learned that Micah had hired a Levite of Bethlehem to be the priest at his personal temple on Mt. Ephraim. In Chapter 18, we learned that the marauding Danites had hired that Levite away from Micah and brought him, and the idol, along to their conquest of Layish=Dan, where it remained "all the while that the House of God stood at Shiloh" (18:31). What are the odds that there was another Levite on Mt. Ephraim with links to Bethlehem?

Moreover, we even know this Levite's name: "Jonathan son of Gershom son of Me^{n}asheh" (18:30). I have attempted to replicate the Scriptural representation of his name—i.e., with the letter *nun* in suspension—to highlight a rabbinic interpretation that eliminates the suspended letter from the text, leaving only *m-sh-h*, thereby identifying him as the grandson of none other than Moses himself.

Lest we reject that out of hand, recall that in Chapters 17 and 18 we called attention to the rabbinic assumption that these events transpired at the beginning of the era of the judges—despite being reported only at the end (a point we plan to address in our retrospective at the end of the book). Consider, additionally, that at a critical moment in the denouement of this episode the people seek divine counsel via a priest whose name is given as "Phinehas son of Elazar, son of Aaron" (20:28).

A third-generation descendant of Moses reunited with a third-generation descendant of Aaron in the selfsame episode. Coincidence?

Judges 20

An Un-Civil War

The rape and degradation of the Levite's concubine by the inhabitants of Gibeah—detailed in the previous chapter and reiterated in vs. 2ff.—have their consequences: a civil war erupts, pitting the tribe of Benjamin—standing up for their own members—against "the balance of the tribes of Israel" numbering some 400,000 (2). Although vastly outnumbered (the Benjaminites numbered but 26,000 plus the 700 left-handed sharpshooters we referred to back in Chapter 3), they managed to take out 10 percent of their opponents (22,000 in v. 21 and another 18,000 in v. 25). It is at this juncture that the Israelites sought divine counsel via Phinehas the Priest, as we mentioned in the previous chapter.

With Phinehas's assent, the Israelites set up ambushes about Gibeah. They pretended to be routed, drawing the defenders out of the city (32). Then they sprang their trap, catching the Benjaminites betwixt and between (33–34), slaying 25,100 of them (35): 18,000 in the field of battle (44), 5,000 more on the wilderness road, and 2,000 near Gid'om (45).

If you do the math, that adds up to 25,000, which is what v. 46 reports. Recalling, however, that v. 35 reported total losses at 25,100, we may side with either Rashi, who implied that the remaining 100 were omitted from the total because they were killed in unspecified locations, or with Radak, whose opinion was that Scripture rounded off the total to the nearest thousand. Since the total Benjaminite army was reported earlier as 26,700, that would leave between 1,600 and 1,700 survivors, but v. 47 reports that only 600 soldiers took refuge in Rimon Rock, leaving us to speculate about the fate of the remaining 1,000.

Whatever their exact number, the final chapter of the Book of Judges, which follows anon, presumes that only males survived, leaving the victors to confront an unanticipated result of their triumph: the possible demise of an entire tribe.

Judges 21

It Wasn't Sadie Hawkins Day at Shiloh

The Mishnah declares:

> No festivals were as joyous to Israel as 15 Av and Yom HaKippurim, on which the young women of Jerusalem would turn out in borrowed white clothes in order not to embarrass anyone who had no [finery] of their own.... They would dance in the vineyards calling to the young men: Look up and choose! Pay no mind to wealth but to family... (*Ta'anit* 4:8).

While the dates were chosen for symbolic value—on 15 Av, the last of the generation that was fated to die in the wilderness passed on, and Yom HaKippurim, the day on which the second set of tablets was delivered, marked the start of Israel's redemption after the sin of the golden calf—the pageant itself seems to be patterned after the events described in this, the closing chapter of the Book of Judges.

As we noted at the close of the previous chapter, the few surviving Benjaminites were facing extinction as a tribe because of two factors: The first, implicit, is that only men survived the civil war, and the second, explicit, was that the remaining tribes took an oath not to give their daughters in marriage to Benjaminites (1). When the Israelites experienced regret over this alarming prospect, they resorted to a legal circumvention: Since the inhabitants of Jabesh-Gilead were not present when the oath was taken, they were technically not bound by it, so 400 of their unmarried women were given to the Benjaminites.

However, since there were at least 600 (and perhaps as many as 1,000) Benjaminite men who needed wives—as we calculated at the end of the previous chapter—another stratagem had to be adopted. The Benjaminites were advised to set up an ambush (the very same strategy that had been their undoing at Gibeah, cf. 20:29), and when the young women of Shiloh came out to dance in the vineyards, they were to take them to be their wives.

Not at all an acceptable strategy from the perspective of an age of #MeToo, but clearly passable in that early patriarchal era.

Retrospective on Judges: Themes and Variations

In our comments over the last four chapters of the Book of Judges, we had occasion to report on the rabbinic view that the book does not maintain a strict chronological sequence and that the events described in its concluding section actually transpired at the very start of the era. Here, we should like to suggest that this is because an alternative organizational principle was utilized for the book: a thematic one. We are indebted to the authors and editors of the *Da'at Mikra* series for their inspiration.

Part one, covering through 2:5, informs us that the source of all evils during this period was the neglect of Joshua's instructions to complete the conquest of the land and, paradoxically, forging alliances with the indigenous nations against whose company they were warned going back to Moses and the Torah.

Part two, extending through Chapter 16, apprises us that the most serious consequence of that neglect was idolatry, adopting the mores of the people they had failed to evict from the land. Each time their negligence reached a high-water mark, they were delivered into the hands of an enemy, their oppression lasting until they rallied around a religious savior and the waters that threatened to engulf them receded, albeit temporarily.

Part three, comprising the final five chapters, serves as the book's conclusion, describing perhaps the most egregious events pertaining to the themes of idolatry and depravity, regardless of their place in the chronological sequence. It is itself divisible into Chapters 17–18 and 19–21. The first tells of Micah's idol and delivers a somewhat sarcastic rebuke for idolatry that was so ongoing that it blithely utilized monies dedicated to God and employed a Levite as priest. The second is more austere and severe, depicting the anti-social behavior of Gibeah on a par with that of the infamous Sodom and Gomorrah, leaving a legacy of civil strife and near devastation due, again, to the influence of their assimilation of local mores and habits.

The concluding verse of the book, a repetition of "in those days there was no king in Israel," links the two halves of the final portion to one another and serves as a segue into the Book of Samuel, as we shall shortly see.

First Samuel

Frank William Warwick Topham,
Samuel Dedicated by Hannah

1 Samuel 1

A New Era Starts with the "Same Old"

Moses received the Torah at Sinai and transferred it to Joshua. Joshua [transferred it] to the elders, the elders to the prophets, and the prophets transferred it to the Men of the Great Assembly (*Avot* 1:1).

Having passed from the Torah (Moses) through the Books of Joshua and Judges ("the elders"), we enter the era of the prophets with the Book of Samuel.

Some of what we read at the beginning of this book is familiar. Once again, our lead character, Elkanah, lives on Mt. Ephraim, and, once again, there are traces of a link to Bethlehem (see our comments to Judges 17 and 19) in his designation as Ephrati (1), a title used elsewhere to identify natives of Bethlehem (cf. Ruth 1:2). On the other hand, he is married to two women—far fewer than several of the judges who had to have been married to numerous women in order to father their scores of children. Likewise, in a narrative manner reminiscent of the birth of Moses (Exodus 2), the father (here—Elkanah, there—Amram) recedes far into the background, leaving the women (here—Hannah and Peninah, there—Jochebed and Miriam) to dictate the course of events.

Of particular interest here is the nature of the relationship between Elkanah's wives as described in verse 6: "And her rival vexed her sore, to make her fret (*har'imah*), because the Lord had shut up her womb" (JPS 1917), which can be read in two completely different ways. According to the conventional reading, Peninah mocked Hannah's infertility increasing her despair. This is reflected in the first half of

Rashi's commentary: "She would say to her, 'Did you buy your older son a cloak today, or your younger son, a shirt?'" The unconventional reading, however, reflected in the continuation of that same commentary, imputes to Peninah a nobler intent: "In order to make her complain. Our Rabbis explain (*Bava Batra* 16a), 'in order to make her storm (*ra'am*),' that she prays. Peninah had good intentions."

So, our hero, Samuel, seems to be the product of a kind of domestic tension we have seen previously. First, it matches the circumstances out of which Isaac emerged: a patriarchal father figure (Abraham), a favorite wife who is without child (Sarah), and a second wife (Hagar) whose fecundity makes a mockery of her rival's infertility. And it is also reminiscent of the situation of Jacob whose favorite, Rachel, was vexed by the fertility of her rival, Leah.

New lyrics, but an old melody.

1 Samuel 2

Hannah's Prayer and Kingship

In the previous chapter, Hannah's request of God for a child is repeatedly called a prayer (10, 12, 27). Here, her thanksgiving song in celebration of his birth is identified the same way (1). Small wonder, then, that the Talmud (*Berakhot, passim*) regards Hannah's prayer as so exemplary that it becomes a paradigm for Jewish prayer in general.

A quick perusal of that song reveals that up to the end of its final verse, its theme, fittingly, is the reversal of fortunes. Just as the childless Hannah was blessed with a son ("the barren bore seven," 5), so can the poor anticipate riches (7–8), the pious can expect rescue from the hands of the wicked (9), and even the dead can foresee resurrection (according to an admittedly clumsy reading of v. 6: "The Lord takes life and [then] grants it").

The conclusion, however, appears to be out of sorts. How does the birth of Samuel connect with "He will give strength unto His king, and exalt the strength of His anointed" (10)?

And while we are inquiring into dissonant elements in the narrative, why is the uplifting saga of Samuel's birth followed immediately by the dispiriting notice that "Eli's sons were ignoble men who knew not the Lord" (12)?

Since our reading of Samuel follows that of Judges, we already have an answer that will address both our questions. In our retrospective on the Book of Judges, we commented:

> The concluding verse of the book, a repetition of "In those days there was no king in Israel," links the two halves of the final portion [of Judges] to one another and also serves as a segue into the Book of Samuel, as we shall shortly see.

Samuel was destined to be the catalyst to redress the state of anarchy into which he was born, hence his mother's (intuitive? prophetic?) allusion to an Israelite king ("His anointed"). The reference to Eli's sons' contemptibility, on the other hand, is a foreshadowing of Samuel's inability to appoint his own sons as his successors on account of their base character ("his sons walked not in his ways, but turned aside after unjust gain, and took bribes, and perverted justice," 8:3). Thus, God instructed him to coronate Saul as Israel's first king (Chapter 9).

1 Samuel 3

His Master's Voice

Our chapter recounts Samuel's first prophetic experience. He mistook the voice of God for that of Eli—not once or even twice but three times—responding, in each case, *hinneni*, "here I am," exactly as the Patriarch Abraham responded to God's summons in Genesis 22:1 and Moses at the burning bush (Exodus 3:4). Eli explained to his charge that God was calling him and that he should acknowledge Him and request his instructions, and so he does—the fourth time around.

While Scripture is silent on the question of exactly how those summonses were issued, it provides us with enough information for some informed speculation.

First, it tells us that in each of the misinterpreted instances, Samuel presented himself to Eli, which implies that Samuel identified the voice of the summons with that of his priestly mentor. The fact that he continued to respond to Eli after discovering—not once but twice—that Eli had not summoned him only strengthens our assumption that the voice calling out "Samuel" sounded like Eli's because no other facts fit the situation.

Our first conclusion, then, is that when God communicated with people, He utilized familiar voices they could readily identify as being those of authority.

A second observation attaches to Eli's reactions. The first time his reply is terse and, perhaps, even pointed: "Go *back* to bed" (5). The second time, however, the "go back to bed" is softened by the addition of "my son" (6). It seems to be dawning on Eli that more is afoot here than just a restless novice, and by the third time his reply is "go to bed" (9), as though the clock were being entirely reset.

A final observation attaches to the summons itself. While the first two times the voice called "Samuel" but once, the third time it called "Samuel Samuel" (10), the duplication of the name reminiscent of the doubled "Abraham Abraham" of Genesis 22:11 and the summons of "Moses Moses" at the burning bush (Exodus 3:4).

# FIRST SAMUEL

1 Samuel 4

Saving the Worst for Last

In this chapter, we learn of the fateful battle with the Philistines at Aphek that ended with the routing of the Israelite army, the deaths of thirty thousand Israelite soldiers—including the two sons of Eli, Hofni and Phinehas—and the capture of the divine Ark (10–11).

If you look carefully, you will notice that the order in which these results are arranged is similar—but not identical in all respects—to two other reports that appear in this chapter. The survivor of the debacle first reported to Eli that "Israel has been routed before the Philistines, suffered a grievous plague, your two sons, Hofni and Phinehas, have died, and the divine Ark was taken" (17). According to the Scriptural narrative, it was only upon hearing of the fate of the Ark that Eli fell off his chair and died, suggesting that the reporter had (compassionately?) left the worst news for last and implying that Eli was affected more by that capture than by the news of his personal loss. [Note, too, the substitution of the euphemistic "suffered a grievous plague" for the actual accounting of KIAs (killed in action)].

When the news is subsequently relayed to Phinehas's pregnant wife, with the additional notice of the death of Eli, the sequence changed: "When she heard the news that the divine Ark was captured, that her father-in-law had died, and so did her husband" (19), she went into premature labor and died in childbirth. Eli's loss was more national and spiritual; hers was acutely more personal.

1 Samuel 5

Spielberg's Muse?

In one of the final scenes of *Raiders of the Lost Ark*, the Ark unleashes grotesque ghost-like figures that cause death to all about them. Was this just artistic license or could it have a basis in Scripture?

In this brief chapter, we learn about the Ark's impact on the Philistines who kept it after its capture. First, it struck down the statue of Dagon in Ashdod (the same god whose temple in Gaza was brought down by Samson, cf. Judges 16), but the Philistines paid it no mind (3). Then it knocked it down again, this time causing its head and hands to fall off, while the general population was smitten with hemorrhoids (3-4). It was then moved to Gat, whose population was likewise stricken with hemorrhoids (10), so it was moved to Ekron, where yet another outbreak of hemorrhoids occurred (12). The only resolution the Philistines offered was to return the Ark whence it came (11) lest it cause a pandemic. In their own words: "Let it go back to its own place, that it slays us not, and our people" (11).

Two things about the divine manner of the Philistines' chastisement are noteworthy. First, God delivered a warning before unleashing the grievous plague. It was the obtuseness of the Philistines, who attributed no significance to the initial fall of the Dagon statue, which necessitated a second round of punishment. Secondly, God struck both Dagon and its worshippers just as He had earlier struck both the gods of Egypt and their worshippers (Exodus 12:12), in order to demonstrate the futility of their idolatry.

Whether *Raiders'* director Steven Spielberg or its writer Lawrence Kasdan took any note of our chapter cannot be determined, but his insinuation that tampering with the Ark unleashed malign forces is consistent with our reading.

1 Samuel 6

The Ark Comes Home

Seven months after the events described in the previous chapter, the Philistines eventually awakened to the fact that their misfortunes were the result of keeping the Ark, and they decided to return it. To further propitiate the God of Israel, whom they had offended, they sent along gifts. Both the manner of the Ark's return and the nature of those gifts deserve further attention.

As to the return, the Philistine priests and magicians seem to have been intent on challenging the assumption that the Ark was, indeed, responsible for their bad luck, so they contrived to have it placed on a wagon drawn by inexperienced beasts (i.e., no prior inclination to a particular path) and without a driver so that it would return to Israel only if a higher force so directed it. This is indicative of the obstinacy of the Philistines who, despite all the deaths and inconveniences they and their gods had suffered (see our comments to Chapter 5), were yet loath to acknowledge the inadequacies of their own beliefs.

More striking, though, are the presents they sent along: "Five golden hemorrhoids, and five golden mice, according to the number of the lords of the Philistines; for one plague was on you all, and on your lords" (4). Recall—from the previous chapter—that the chastisement the Philistines suffered on account of their capture of the Ark included a plague of hemorrhoids. In the same manner that a folk remedy for a hangover is another drink, they intuited a link between their suffering and its cause and imagined that surrendering these golden objects would provide atonement for their disrespect to the Ark and its Master.

The unguided wagon and its precious cargo ended up at the field of an inhabitant of Beit Shemesh named Joshua (!), where "they cleaved the wood of the cart, and offered up the cows for a burnt-offering unto the Lord" (14), and yet God "smote of the men of Beit Shemesh, because they had gazed upon the ark of the Lord" (19). Significantly, the Torah includes a warning to the Levites "lest they glimpse the sacred [vessels of the Tabernacle] as they are being covered and die" (Numbers 4:20).

1 Samuel 7

A Liquid Libation before the Lord

The fact that God smote the people of Beit Shemesh after they retrieved the Ark indicates that they regarded its return by the Philistines as somewhat less than an unmitigated blessing, leading to their decision to transfer it to Kiryat Ye'arim. There, it seems to have been accorded greater respect as signified, perhaps, by its placement in the house of Abinadab "on the hilltop" and the "sanctification" of a special caretaker (1). Hence, the observation that the next twenty years were marked by an ongoing commitment to God (2).

And yet the syncretistic form of worship—combining elements of the genuine service of God with local superstitions—that we have taken note of previously (see our comments on Judges 17) persevered, and Samuel had to call upon them to repent by ridding themselves of their "foreign deities" and to serve "God alone" (3). He appears to have succeeded because when the Philistines next challenge Israel, at Mitzpah, he led them in prayer to God, Who heard their plea for His intercession and granted them victory.

One detail of their process of repentance is noteworthy. We read that "they gathered together to Mitzpah, drew water, poured it out before the Lord, fasted on that day, and said there: 'We have sinned against the Lord'" (6). While fasting is a recognizable feature of the process of seeking atonement, what was the significance of pouring water?

An original answer was provided by R. Yosef Ibn Kaspi (Provence, 1279–1340): "They poured water over their location, as well as over their faces and hands, to impress upon their souls that they were cleansed of their defilement." Pointedly, drawing water also serves as a symbol of redemption, as in a well-known verse used in the Havdalah ceremony: "Draw water joyfully from the wellsprings of salvation" (Isaiah 12:3).

1 Samuel 8

Sometimes the Apple Does Fall Far from the Tree

Samuel's sons, like Eli's before him, were unfit to succeed their father. Eli allowed Hofni and Phinehas to serve as priests, and they took advantage of their parishioners (2:12ff.); Samuel appointed Joel and Abiyah as judges in a Beersheba district court, and they used their positions to solicit bribes (3). In consequence thereof, the people clamored for a king in order to resemble all the surrounding nations (5). Samuel viewed their request with disfavor, appearing to take it personally, but God reassured him that it was He the people were rejecting, not the prophet (7), and acquiesced in their demand (9). There follows a long diatribe by Samuel enumerating the likely excesses of a monarchy (11–18) but the people were persistent (19) and God, too, affirmed their request (22).

Several questions present themselves here:

1. Why would the people expect Samuel's sons to succeed him when the principle of succession was not a fixture of the era of the Judges?
2. If the issue was succession, and both Eli and Samuel had already failed at it, why did they expect a monarchy to solve it?
3. Since the Torah already made provision for a king (Deut. 17:14ff.), why did both Samuel and God view the request negatively?

First, we need to acknowledge that there was an active principle of succession already in force in respect of the priesthood. It could be that its weakening after Eli's sons made it suspect and that its further deterioration after Samuel's sons was the last straw. The reason we never saw it implemented during the era of the judges may simply be that since so many of them had such extensive tenures (20 years, 40 years), by the time they needed to be replaced their sons may have been otherwise successfully occupied and uninterested in public service.

Second, it may not have been the failure of succession, per se, that was disturbing but the confusion and uncertainty that it had caused. Dynastic succession may simply have appeared longer lasting and more stable.

As to the Torah's prior provision for monarchy and, yet, God's disinclination towards it, this is the subject of extensive speculation from the Talmud through the medieval exegetes. To cite but one representative opinion, here is part of the comment of Radak:

> Because they demanded it in the form of a grievance (*tar'omet*) rather than in fulfillment of a mitzvah. Had they said, "Give us a king to judge us justly and righteously," Samuel would not have disagreed because his own sons were unjust magistrates.

FIRST SAMUEL

1 Samuel 9

Samuel and Saul: The Seer and The Seen

Some years ago, I started a public lecture on 1 Samuel by asserting that Samuel and Saul were switched at birth. It caught the audience's attention, as I had expected, but then I had to elaborate. I drew their attention to Chapter One, verses 27–28, in which Hannah explained to Eli: "I prayed for this child. God granted me the request I asked of him. So, I have put him on loan to God; all the days of his being he will be on loan to God."

The verbal root *SH-'-L*, "to request or to borrow," repeats itself no fewer than four times in these two verses, most prominently in the concluding phrase which, taken quite literally, actually says "all the days of his being he will be *sha'ul* to God." There you have it: Hannah's son was intended to be Shaul; since he turned out, instead, to be Samuel, they must have been switched at birth.

Let us look at the circumstances in which Samuel and Saul first met. Saul's father had lost some donkeys and dispatched Saul and one of his servants to seek them. Just as Saul was about to give up, the servant suggested a visit to Samuel. At first glance, this appears odd. Samuel was a circuit judge and a prophet, but not a lost and found. The servant, however, knew otherwise; he referred to Samuel as "the man of God" (6), and even produced what seems to have been the price of admission for an audience with him: a silver quarter (8).

The critical verse follows: "Aforetime in Israel, when a man went to inquire of God, he would say: 'Come and let us go to the seer'; for he that is now called a prophet was aforetime called a seer" (9). The association of prophecy (*navi*) with seeing (*ro'eh*) is reinforced by our observation that prophetic communication is oftentimes called a sight (*mar'eh*) and, otherwise, a vision (*hazon*).

But whose words are these? Rashi inferred that they were not spoken by Saul's servant but were interpolated by "the scribe (*sofer*) who wrote the Book of Samuel." Radak elaborated on the seeming incongruity of "aforetime" when this encounter occurred shortly before the deaths of both protagonists and explained that "aforetime" refers to an earlier era in which prophets were known for the ability to foretell events or disclose hidden things. By the era of Samuel, however, the definition had evolved to identify a *navi* as an interlocutor (*niv sefatayim*): one who bore divine messages to the people.

1 Samuel 10

Where is Rachel's Tomb?

At the close of the previous chapter, Samuel took Saul aside and intimated that he had something to tell him. As this chapter opens, we learn that the message he sought to convey to him was that God had chosen him to rule over Israel (1). Samuel continued, however, and delivered to Saul a somewhat enigmatic instruction:

> When you leave me today, you will find two men by the tomb (*kevurat*) of Rachel, near the border of Benjamin at Zelzah. They will say to you: The donkeys that you went to seek have been found, and your father has ceased caring for the donkeys, and is anxious about you, asking: What shall I do about my son? (2)

Implicit in Samuel's instructions (which also mention Bethel and allude to Kiryat Ye'arim) is that Zelzah is north of Jerusalem. Recall, too, a famous verse: "Hark! A bitter cry can be heard in the Ramah. Rachel is mourning the loss of her children" (Jeremiah 31:14). An otherwise unspecified Ramah (literally, "heights") usually refers to the home of Samuel—likewise north of Jerusalem. In Genesis 35:19–20, however, Rachel's death is set "on the road to Ephrat, which is Bethlehem" south of Jerusalem, and Jacob erected a monument over her tomb (*kevurat*) that is visible "to this very day," as any visitor to Bethlehem can attest.

This very conundrum confounded Ramban (Nahmanides, 1194–1270). In his Torah commentary (to Genesis 35:16), he originally wrote that Rachel's tomb is situated at some (unspecified) distance from Bethlehem. After his arrival in the Land of Israel (c. 1267), however, he added:

> This is what I thought previously. Now that I have merited to come to Jerusalem, praise to the beneficent God, I can see with my own two eyes that the distance between Rachel's' tomb (*kevurat*) and Bethlehem is less than a mile, contradicting my original interpretation.

Regardless of where Rachel was buried, Saul was a Benjaminite and, assumedly, held the tomb of his ancestress in singular regard. By directing him there, Samuel may have been inviting him to connect with his tribal roots and, perhaps, to draw from them the strength and support he would need to initiate and sustain his rule.

My personal inclination is to identify *kevurat Rachel* with the Muslim shrine called Nebi Samwil situated on an elevation just north of Jerusalem ("near the border of Benjamin"), regarded as the burial site of the Prophet Samuel. Since Samuel's Ramah was further north, in the Ephraim hill country in which he was born, it is possible that Muslim tradition got the two confused.

IN THE COMPANY OF PROPHETS

1 Samuel 11

Saul, Champion of Israel

Although Samuel had all but promised Saul the kingship, and although his selection was made at God's behest, Saul still lacked the popular acceptance that would cement his rule. This chapter tells us how that transpired.

The citizens of Jabesh-Gilead were threatened by the Ammonites, and they sought a champion (*moshi'a*) to fight for their cause (3). Saul was upset by the news of their plight, and he received a divine inspiration (6) that led him to gather an army of 330,000 soldiers (8). (Bear in mind that the IDF standing force is only about 200,000.) By dividing his forces into three parts, he was able to infiltrate the Ammonite lines and rout them so thoroughly that "not even two remain[ed] together" (12).

The Gilead region was in Trans-Jordan; could they find no closer assistance than Benjamin? Indeed, they "sent throughout the borders of Israel" (3) in search of a champion, implicitly drawing no response. Why, then, did Saul enlist? Recalling Judges 21, Jabesh-Gilead was the only place that had not participated in the ban on marrying Benjaminites, and the prospect of the eventual elimination of that entire tribe was forestalled by forcibly taking 400 women from Jabesh-Gilead and giving them in marriage to Benjaminites. Is it possible that Saul was the product of such a marriage and was, as it were, repaying a debt?

Speculation aside, the result of Saul's overwhelming victory is precisely the affirmation of monarchic rule that was absent heretofore. "And the people said unto Samuel: Anyone who says: Is Saul fit to reign over us? Turn them over and we will put them to death" (12).

Saul declared, magnanimously, "No one will die today, for today has been a day of divine deliverance" (13), and Samuel, taking his cue, declared to the people: "Let us go to Gilgal and inaugurate the monarchy" (14). They went there and coronated Saul amidst great festivity (15) and, at least for the time being, everything seemed satisfactory.

1 Samuel 12

Don't Rain on My Harvest

In his attempt to consolidate Saul's rule, Samuel reiterated the principle that the fate of Israel is inextricably tied to the sincerity of their worship of God (see our comments on Judges 2) and offered them a truly convincing sign ("this great thing," 16) of its veracity:

> Is it not the wheat harvest today? I will call unto the Lord that He may send thunder and rain, and you shall know and see that you have done a great wickedness in the sight of the Lord by asking for a king. (17)

The fact that he succeeded and "all the people greatly feared the Lord and Samuel" (18) only intensifies our perplexity: What is so impressive about rain? Radak, although he lived in Provence, appreciated the proof:

> My father, *z"l*, explained that in the Land of Israel rain does not fall at all during the harvest…. Our sages have said that the 17th of *Marheshvan* [in the fall] starts the rainy season. Since rain during the harvest season was a great novelty for them, they took fear and asked Samuel to pray for them lest they die.

According to Nogah Hareuveni, a leading scholar in the field of botany and the Bible [*Nature in Our Biblical Heritage*], the period of *sefirat ha-omer* is intended to coincide with the wheat harvest in April and early May. This brief transitional season between the rainy winter and the hot, dry summer is one of erratic and unpredictable weather; one day can bring scorching winds from the desert, the next day, thunder, lightning, and heavy rains.

During this spring season, seven critically important varieties of grain and fruit (Israel's "seven species") are all particularly vulnerable stages of development. The olive, grape, pomegranate, and date flowers need several successive days of hot weather to open and be pollinated. Wheat and barley, on the other hand, need cool, moist air. The fiery *hamsin* typical of this season can parch and completely destroy the entire grain crop if it comes before the kernels have filled with starch. The same rains that benefit the wheat and barley during their last stages of ripening can devastate the fruit crop. In order to survive, people needed both the grain and the fruit.

Not surprising, then, that this period would be one of high anxiety and trepidation and suitable for Samuel's object lesson.

1 Samuel 13

The Real Saul

Several questions present themselves apropos of this chapter, but all are addressed by one or another of the classic exegetes.

First of all, the very first verse challenges us by stipulating that "Saul was one year old when he reigned, and he reigned over Israel for two years." As precocious as he may have been, a literal reading of the verse is, of course, out of the question. Rashi, typically, offered two interpretations. The midrashic one takes "one year old" as a metaphor for innocence ("he had not tasted sin") and the more prosaic one reads the verse as "Saul reigned for two years. In the first year... [continue with verse 2]." Ralbag (Gersonides), extending Rashi's interpretation, related this verse to Saul's earlier trouble in consolidating his monarchy (see our comments on Chapters 11–12), reading it as: one year had already elapsed between his inauguration by Samuel until the acclamation of his sovereignty at Gilgal.

The second question is: Since it was Saul's ongoing intention to combat the Philistines, why did he demobilize the large army that had fought successfully (in Chapter 12), winnowing it to a mere three thousand? Ralbag assumed that the three thousand were elite soldiers who, arguably, could have been sent into action at a moment's notice, while the rest were mobilized as reserves (much as the current IDF practice). Malbim, on the other hand, took the reduction in forces to indicate either that Saul had not yet resolved to go to war or that it was customary for kings to take a "year off" at the start of their reigns in order to see to domestic affairs before embarking on more adventurous undertakings.

More poignant, however, is the insight we obtain into Saul's true self from his behavior in Gilgal on the eve of battle. Samuel had—implicitly—instructed Saul to await his arrival before offering sacrifices for their victory (8), but Saul hastened to offer the sacrifices in the prophet's absence (9), justifying his actions by arguing "the people were dispersing" (11). Saul was, by objective description, statuesque (9:2, "head and shoulders above the rest"), but he suffered from extreme self-consciousness and was reluctant to use his physical advantage to enforce his authority. On a previous occasion, he had "hidden amongst the vessels" (10:22) rather than exercise leadership and here, too, he declined to assert himself despite Samuel's instructions, allowing the "people" to determine his actions.

Not surprisingly, Samuel acknowledged this moment as the beginning of Saul's end (14), and we await the denouement in chapter 15.

IN THE COMPANY OF PROPHETS

1 Samuel 14

Saul Consolidated the Monarchy, And...?

There are so many items of interest in this chapter that it was quite a challenge to single out only one for comment.

Just a glimpse of the proverbial road not taken would include, first, the array of delightful place names such as Migron (2), Botzetz & Seneh (4), and Michmash (5). The chapter also encompasses the episode of Jonathan and his armor bearer's commando raid against the Philistines (6ff.) and how they successfully employed an early form of psy-ops (9ff.). Same for their unwitting disobedience to Saul's counterproductive order to abstain from all food (24), his subsequent rash vow to punish any violator "even my son Jonathan" (39, highly reminiscent of Jephthah's rash vow in Judges 11), and how their lives were spared by popular acclaim (45).

What I have chosen to focus on is verse 47: "Saul consolidated the monarchy over Israel and fought against all his enemies on all sides: Moab, Ammon, Edom, the kings of [Aram] Zobah, and the Philistines; and wherever he turned, *yarshi'a*."

I have deliberately left the last word untranslated because that is the crux of the matter. While a host of medieval exegetes and English translations have labored mightily to turn it to Saul's advantage (e.g., King James: "he vexed them," English Standard: "he routed them," JPS: "he put them to the worse"), the undeniable fact is that the Hebrew literally means "he [Saul] was wicked." While "wicked" (from the Old English *wicca*, meaning "wizard") has the slang meaning of excellent, the Hebrew *rasha'* does not.

The sole exception to this history of interpretation (and not for the only time) was Malbim (1809–1879), who manipulated grammar to his advantage. He substituted the object of the sentence for its subject and attached it to the following verse, yielding (in paraphrase): Saul fought against all these enemies. Indeed, in whatever direction a wicked one (i.e., an external enemy) confronted him, he acted valiantly.

1 Samuel 15

Who Tore Whose Cloak?

Samuel instructed Saul to exact Israel's vengeance against its arch-foe, Amalek, and to be pitiless in its pursuit. Saul, true to form, disobeyed his instructions, leaving Agag, the Amalekite king, alive, and sparing the choicest sheep and cattle (9). When Samuel rebuked him (14ff.), he replied, characteristically, that he could not withstand the popular demand (24). Samuel then notified him that his monarchy was coming to an end and Saul, desperate to keep up appearances, asked Samuel to accompany him back to face the people (25), but the prophet declined (26).

Then, "Samuel turned to depart, and *he* seized the corner of *his* cloak and it tore" (27). Hence, the title of our inquiry: Who tore whose cloak? Four logical possibilities can be sustained: Saul tore Samuel's coat, Samuel tore his own coat, Saul tore his own coat, and Samuel tore Saul's coat. It is my opinion that Saul tore Samuel's coat as he was turning to depart because the passive "it tore" (*va-yikkara'*) implies an accidental tearing and the other three possibilities require deliberate action. While only this explanation, of the four, conveys the accidental value of "it was torn," the problem is that without the interpolation of a new subject (Saul) into the sentence, the verb "he seized" is still governed by Samuel. Our solution: Saul had already taken hold of Samuel's coat, and is therefore already recognized as the implicit subject of all subsequent actions performed on it. We have two proofs to submit in evidence.

First of all, the verse employs neither the verb *a-h-z* nor *t-f-s*—either of which would simply mean "to take hold, or grasp" (as in 1 Kings 11:30)—rather it uses *ch-z-k*, which, strictly speaking, means to strengthen an existing grip. This implies that Saul had already taken hold of Samuel's coat and, when Samuel was threatening to abandon him, Saul tightened his hold. Hence, the second proof: At the beginning of the encounter, Saul had greeted Samuel with the claim of: "I have upheld the word of God" (13), to which Samuel countered: "What is this bleating of sheep in my ears?" (14), which Saul tried to excuse as "intended for sacrifice" (15). Samuel then said to Saul: "Let go of me" (*heref*; or, "stay your hand," as JPS itself translates in 2 Samuel 24:16), implying that Saul had previously taken hold of Samuel's coat.

1 Samuel 16

Nothing but the Truth?

Samuel was so invested in Saul's monarchy that he was literally in mourning over its loss. God basically told him to get over it and ordered him to Bethlehem to anoint a yet unnamed son of Jesse to succeed Saul. Samuel complained: "How can I go? If Saul hears of it, he will have me killed." God replied: "Take along a calf and say you are going to offer a sacrifice to God" (2).

This verse features prominently in the following talmudic passage (*Yevamot* 65b):

> Ile'a further stated in the name of R. Eleazar son of R. Simeon: One may (*mutar*) modify a statement (*leshanot*) in the interests of peace, for it is said in Scripture, "Your father commanded before his death, so shall you say to Joseph:

Please forgive your brothers' wrongdoing," etc.* R. Nathan said: It is a commandment (*mitzvah*), for it is stated in Scripture, "And Samuel said: 'How can I go? If Saul hears it, he will kill me'" etc.

Note, first and foremost, that the Talmud does not solicit or condone outright lying (*leshaker*), only being evasive. Since Samuel indeed prepared for a sacrifice (5), which became the "cover" under which he met the sons of Jesse and discovered young David, he was telling the truth. Perhaps, in this case, it was not the whole truth, but surely it was nothing but the truth.

*Genesis 50: 16. There is no textual evidence that Jacob gave these instructions to his sons, allowing for the insinuation that the words, designed to appease Joseph and preserve household harmony, were their own.

1 Samuel 17

David I and David II

While the one-on-one combat between David and Goliath—featured in this chapter—is known well-nigh universally, some of its lesser known features are well worth a second look.

Let us begin with the inconsistency between David's introduction to Saul as a musician, reported in the previous chapter (16:18ff.), and his appearance in this chapter as a prospective champion (31ff.). After his victory, Saul turned to his Chief of Staff, Abner ben Ner, and asked, "Who is this young man's father?" to which Abner replied, "I honestly don't know" (55), forcing Saul to ask David directly (58). While it is true that Saul was reported (in chapter 16) to undergo mood swings—and we will see his attitude towards David changing as well—how could he have failed to recognize his favorite lute player?

Even more striking, perhaps, is the common misapprehension regarding David's age and physical stature at the time of his encounter with Goliath. Rather than a callow youth of relatively diminutive stature, there is textual evidence that he was above average height and in his late twenties. Let us go to the verses:

> And Saul clad David with his apparel, put a helmet of brass upon his head, and clad him with a coat of mail. And David girded his sword upon his apparel and tried (*va-yo'el*) to go [but could not], for he had not tried it (*ki lo nissah*). And David said to Saul: "I cannot go with these, for I have not tried them." And David removed them. (38–39)

Simply put, Saul tried to give David the advantage of a suit of armor, but David, who was not an experienced soldier, found that it restricted his movements, so he removed it. But it is not all that simple. Recall that Saul was "head and shoulders above all the people" (9:2), implying that if he thought David could wear his armor, then David had to be of a comparable size. Recall, as well, that Saul reigned for only two years (13:1); since David was 30 years old when he ascended the throne (2 Samuel 5:4), he had to have been about 28 or 29 years old when he fought Goliath.

Indeed, Radak rejected the simple reading of v. 39, "for I have not tried them," favoring "for it would be no miracle" (*nissah=nes*), explaining that if David had fought while dressed and armed as a regular soldier, it would have diminished the miraculous nature of his victory.

FIRST SAMUEL

1 Samuel 18

Beware of Poetic License

David's defeat of Goliath and subsequent routing of the Philistines was lauded by the women of Israel in song, with lyrics such as "Saul smote thousands, and David—tens of thousands" (7). Saul was greatly vexed and stated, "They have awarded David tens of thousands and me [only] thousands; next [they will award him] the kingdom" (8). Was Saul, who was, after all, the king and entitled to some preferential treatment, justified in his jealousy?

Let us take a moment to review what we know about biblical poetry. Rather than being governed by such features as rhyme and meter—although they do occasionally exist—biblical poems are characterized by their use of parallelism: the employment of synonymous nouns and verbs in the two respective halves of a poetic measure. A classic illustration is Deut. 32:1: "Hearken heavens as I speak, listen earth to my words." While heaven and earth are clearly not identical, they serve as poetic synonyms all the same, signifying everywhere.

Other such pairs include "tent" and "tabernacle" (Numbers 24:5), "evening" and "morning" (Ps. 30:6), and, of course, "thousands" and "tens of thousands." (In Hebrew, "thousands" and "tens of thousands" are each one word: *alafim* and *revavot*, so the parallelism is clearer in the original than in translation.) Tents and tabernacles both signify places of residence, evening and morning are moments in time, and thousands and tens of thousands mean many.

In other words, the singers' use of these words was not prose, but poetry, and, as such, should not have been taken as literally as Saul clearly took it. Their intention may not have been to aggrandize David tenfold, but to accentuate the myriad accomplishments of both. It was only in Saul's manic state that he read into their song more than they may have intended.

1 Samuel 19

Naked Prophets

When Samuel dispatched Saul home after their initial encounter, one of the signs he gave him to affirm his selection as king was that he would meet a cohort of prophets and would join them in prophesying (10:5–6). When it actually came to pass (10:10ff.), it was so striking that an adage (*mashal*) was coined: "Is Saul, too, a prophet?" (10:12).

In this chapter, that refrain is repeated. After Michal, Saul's daughter and David's wife, aided and abetted David's escape, Saul sent his agents to arrest him. When two groups of agents succumbed to the charms of a cohort of prophets led by Samuel himself, Saul decided to take matters into his own hands, and he set out after David as well. He, too, encountered this cohort of prophets and he, too, joined in their prophesying (23). This time, however, there was a significant departure from precedent: "And he also stripped off his clothes, and he also prophesied before Samuel, and lay down naked all that day and all that night. Wherefore they say: 'Is Saul also among the prophets?'" (24)

The inappropriateness of this behavior was not lost on most of the medieval exegetes who interpreted "his clothes" to be, specifically, his royal garb, which he removed in order to appear no differently from the other prophets. As Rashi wrote: "He removed his royal garments, to put on a disciple's garments."

Radak, however, appreciating that the addition of the word "also" (*gam*) implied that the other prophets had removed their clothes as well, explained the strange activity as follows:

When prophecy overcomes a person, his senses are nullified and he falls down, as it states of Balaam: "He fell down with his eyes open" (Numbers 24:4, 16) and of Daniel: "I was sound asleep, prostrate, with my face in the ground" (10:9). Frequently, it also occurred that he would remove his clothes on account of the nullification of his senses and his conscious thoughts, remaining on an exclusively rational plane.

In other words, since prophecy—according to Maimonides and his followers, including Radak—is the perfection of the intellect, a prophetic state is one in which ordinary, corporeal, sensations, such as the need to be clothed, are overridden.

1 Samuel 20

Jonathan's Psy-Ops and Intel Subterfuges

A good deal of this chapter may be familiar to some readers as the *haftarah* (additional reading for Sabbaths and festivals) for a Shabbat preceding the start of a new lunar month. It was chosen on account of the words "tomorrow is the month" (*mahar hodesh*) with which Jonathan addressed David (18).

A recurring phenomenon in this chapter is how future conduct or behavior is assumed to be revealed through specific actions or words. First, David told Jonathan that he planned to absent himself from the royal table and asked his dear friend to "cover" for him by saying that he was invited home for a family affair. David reasoned that if Saul accepted that excuse for his absence, then he was free and clear; otherwise it signaled that the king's intentions towards him were malign (5ff.).

Next, Jonathan and David contrived a way to get the message to David through a subterfuge. David was to secret himself in a particular place; Jonathan would practice archery nearby, and the manner in which he dispatched his lad to retrieve the arrows would alert David to the king's mood (19ff.).

These incidents are highly reminiscent of an earlier one in which Jonathan and his armor bearer launched their commando-style attack on the Philistines based on how the sentry would challenge them (see our comments to Chapter 14), and to Gideon's predicating his nighttime raid on the Midianites on overhearing the recitation of a dream. In all, the Israelites seem to have been adept at psychologically profiling their adversaries and using that analysis as a basis for predicting their actions and dealing with them.

1 Samuel 21

Am I Short of Fools?

In this brief chapter, we gain additional insight into David's character. He is pragmatic, audacious, and inventive.

His pragmatism is on display as he avoided Saul's posse by seeking refuge with Ahimelech amongst the priests of Nob (2), and he was audacious when he brazenly misrepresented himself to the priest as being on a royal mission (3). He obtained food for his troops—the "showbread" (7)—and even secured arms, at least for himself (10). It is, indeed, curious that Goliath's sword was in the possession of Ahimelech. The last we heard of it—and even that, indirectly—was that David had decapitated Goliath, brought his head to Jerusalem, "and his vessels he placed in his tent" (17:54). Assuming the sword was included among those vessels, it is unclear how it got to Nob, although the fact that it was wrapped up with the ephod, a priestly garment, would indicate that it was kept as a holy treasure, as a memento of the miracle in which it had played a role.

The fleeting reference to the unnoticed presence at Nob of Doeg the Edomite, Saul's head herdsman, serves the literary function of a foreshadowing, whose details are provided in the next chapter (22:9ff.).

David's inventiveness came to the fore when he took on the appearance and behavior of a fool in order to relieve any suspicions that the Philistines of Gath may have entertained about him. Since he was bound to be recognized (if they had post offices, his photo would no doubt have graced every one of them, emblazoned with the legend: "Wanted Dead or Alive"), and, indeed, he was: the Philistines could even recite the words to the song that the Israelite women had composed about him (12). His only recourse was not to deny his identity but to disguise his true self by acting crazy.

The fact that Achish, king of Gath, muttered, "Am I short of fools that you have brought this one to act crazy before me?" (16) may indicate that the presence of fools in Gath was unremarkable and that David had chosen his role well.

1 Samuel 22

Murder at Nob
and the First Conscientious Objection

In our comments on the previous chapter, we noted that the fleeting reference to the unnoticed presence of Doeg the Edomite, Saul's head herdsman, when Ahimelech assisted David in his flight from Saul, foreshadows the events portrayed in this chapter. It was Doeg who "blew the whistle" on the priests of Nob, stirring Saul to call for their deaths. Two unanticipated, perhaps even counterintuitive, details stand out.

First is that Saul's officers refused to participate in wiping out the city of priests. "But the servants of the king would not put forth their hand to fall upon the priests of the Lord" (17). Indeed, the Talmud identifies these officers as Abner ben Ner, the chief of staff, and Amasa ben Yeter, another ranking officer, and states that their refusal stemmed from a legal deliberation that led them to conclude that the order was illegal and had to be defied.* (See Rashi ad loc.)

Both Abner and Amasah were later slain by Joab ben Zeruyah, general of David's army, acts for which that king would hold Joab culpable and which the Talmud relates to the incident at Nob (see our comments on 1 Kings 2).

Second is the description of the way Doeg implemented Saul's order: "Both men and women, children and nursing infants, oxen and donkeys and sheep [were put to death] with the edge of the sword" (19). This is surprising, even frightening, in its tone and detail, the more so when compared with the instructions Samuel issued to Saul to annihilate Amalek: "But slay both men and women, children and nursing infants, oxen and sheep, camels and donkeys" (15:3).

The irony that Saul had failed to implement those earlier instructions (see chapter 15) was not lost on the Sages, who declared that "Nob did not deserve to be treated like Amalek" (*Kohelet Rabbah* 7:16).**

* See Moshe Sokolow, "Disobedience to Military Orders," *Conversations* 15 (2013), 144–153.

** Moshe Sokolow, "Autonomy vs. Heteronomy in Moral Reasoning," *Hazon Nahum* (1997), 659–668.

FIRST SAMUEL

1 Samuel 23

David and the Doubting Thomases

At the beginning of our chapter, the Philistines devastated the Judean town of Keilah by plundering the places to which they would bring their grain for threshing (1). David sought to avenge his people, and he asked God if he would succeed. God replied in the affirmative (2). Then, something odd happened: The Judeans approached David and expressed their fear in the form of a *kal va-chomer* (*a fortiori* argument): "We are afraid here in Judah; how much more so if we go to Keilah against the armies of the Philistines" (3).

Given the earlier divine promise of success, why were they doubtful? Moreover, to allay their fears David renewed his request of God, and God renewed His promise of success (4). This time, the Judeans were reassured, and they joined David in a successful military operation that saved Keilah (5). Why did they accept the second response and not the first?

Malbim answered both questions by means of a very careful parsing of the text. David's initial request and God's first response spoke of smiting Philistines in general (*ba-plishtim*), implying that only a portion of them would be beaten. The second series, however, speaks about beating all the Philistines (*et plishtim*). The Judeans, Malbim explained, were wary of the initial response because they envisioned a situation in which only those who had plundered Keilah would be punished, and the rest of the Philistines would hasten to avenge them. They found the more comprehensive nature of the second inquiry more reassuring.

IN THE COMPANY OF PROPHETS

1 Samuel 24

The Torn Cloak Reprise

In our comments on Chapter 15 ("Who Tore Whose Cloak?"), we concluded that it was Saul who inadvertently tore Samuel's cloak as he grabbed at it to keep the prophet from abandoning him. One of the proofs we offered was that a torn cloak would later become a tangible symbol of Saul's acceptance of David's succession to the monarchy. It is in this chapter that this proof unfolds.

Saul, in the company of 3,000 soldiers, pursued David to the Dead Sea region where David took refuge in one of the caves of Ein Gedi—the general area from which the Dead Sea Scrolls would be recovered millennia later. David sought refuge in the recess of the cave, after which Saul went to sleep near its mouth. Although David could have killed Saul as he slept, he merely cut off a corner of Saul's cloak (4), an act of *lèse majesté* that he subsequently regretted (5–6).

When Saul left the cave, David displayed the torn piece as evidence that Saul's life had been in his hands and he declined to take it (11), invoking an "ancient proverb" (*meshal ha-kadmoni*) to the effect that "evil emanates [only] from the wicked" (13). The sound of David's voice moved Saul to tears (16)—perhaps reminding him of David's earlier lute playing and singing—and he admitted that he had treated David badly (17).

Then Saul made an astonishing admission: "I know that you will surely be king, and that the kingdom of Israel will be established by your hand" (20). What accounted for this sudden acknowledgement that David would be king? Rashi offered two explanations, one *peshat* (contextual) and the second *derash* (homiletic). "[a] For I see that the Holy One, blessed is He, saved you from my hand. [b] The Midrash

Aggadah states that Samuel gave him this sign, that the one who tears his robe will reign after him." With all due deference to Rashi, I think that latter explanation, justified by the larger context, is no less *peshat* than the former.

1 Samuel 25

What's in a Name? Nabal the Scoundrel Meets His End

Samuel's death (another instance of foreshadowing, see 28:3) deprived David of significant backing, and he was forced to take to the wilderness of Paran. Utilizing the 400 indebted and discontented men who had attached themselves to him earlier (22:2), he offered protective services to the locals. In this instance, he solicited a gift from a wealthy sheep rancher of Carmel named Nabal. (This Carmel is situated in the southern Judean hills, not along the northern coastline near Haifa.) Nabal spurned David's request, belittling him ("Who is this David?") and condemning him as a traitorous rebel ("seems to be a rash, nowadays, of rebellious servants" 10). David organized his posse of 400 and set out to teach Nabal a lesson (13).

Enter Abigail, Nabal's wife, who had been described earlier as "of good understanding and of a beautiful form" (3). Apprised by a servant of her husband's perfidy (14ff.), she organized a feast and packed it on donkeys to deliver personally to David (18)—all without her husband's knowledge. When they encountered one another, she implored him to spare her husband, arguing that "he is like his name: he is called Nabal and his behavior is a *nebalah*" (25). While the root *n-b-l* appears many times in Tanakh, we ought to be interested in the particular use of the noun *nebalah*, which describes, inter alia, the rape of Dinah (Genesis 34:7) and the maltreatment of the concubine at Gibeah (Judges 20:6).

Overall, then, *nebalah* describes something outrageous and disgraceful. Abigail was saying "Just look at him; what else would you expect from someone like that?" Whether David was won over by the "goodness of her understanding" or by the "beauty of her form," he relented, and when Nabal died just ten days later of a divinely dispatched death (38), David added her to a growing string of wives.

As we will yet see, again, in 2 Samuel 11, when David became interested in a married woman, her husband's life expectancy was cut short.

1 Samuel 26

Saul's Preoccupation with Paternity and Parentage

Saul Exhibits Here a Greater Paternal Affinity Towards His Erstwhile Nemesis Than He Has Displayed Towards His Own Offspring.

You may recall that there was some ambiguity regarding David's initial introduction to Saul. As we pointed out at that time (Chapters 16–17), David first appeared before Saul as a lute player who succeeded in calming him whenever he was possessed of "an evil spirit" (16:23). It was surprising, then, to discover in the very next chapter that as David defeated Goliath and decapitated him, Saul turned to Abner, his chief of staff, and asked, "Who is this lad's father?", to which Abner replied, "I swear I have no idea" (17:55). When David eventually appeared before Saul, Goliath's head in hand, the king asked him directly and he replied, "I am your servant David son of Jesse the Bethlehemite" (57). Why the emphasis placed on obtaining the name of David's father? While David was assumedly well-known to Saul and his entourage, his remarkable victory over Goliath invited some sort of royal promotion, and that required knowledge of his lineage.

Subsequently, we got another, albeit oblique, glimpse into Saul's preoccupation with parentage when he rebuked his own son Jonathan as a "son of perverse rebellion" who, on account of his friendship with and support for David, was guilty of "shaming your mother's nakedness" (20:30).

In this chapter, we can obtain yet another perspective. While David continued to refer to his relationship with Saul as one of servitude to a master (17, 18, 19), Saul referred to David three times as "my son" (17, 21, 25). Having previously declared David a traitorous rebel and having put a price on his head, Saul now seemed to exhibit a greater paternal affinity towards his erstwhile nemesis than he displayed towards his own offspring.

NB—In addressing Saul, David made a strange accusation against his pursuers, claiming that "[a] they have driven me out this day that I should not cleave unto the inheritance of the Lord, saying: [b] Go, serve other gods" (19). The explicit equivalence between the two halves of the sentence persuaded the Talmud to declare that "Whosoever resides in the Diaspora, resembles one who is godless" (*Ketuvot* 110b).

1 Samuel 27

David the Philistine
Crazy Like a Fox, He Curried Favor with the Enemy.

Why did David still feel threatened by Saul (1) even after the latter (at the end of the previous chapter) had acknowledged David's right to the throne? It may well be that David had diagnosed Saul's malady—as did some of the medieval exegetes—as *marah shechorah* (literally, "black bile"), a euphemism for manic depression, and appreciated that the depressed Saul would not necessarily honor the pledges of his manic self.

Whatever the case, David relocated to the land of the Philistines, despite their being arch-enemies of Israel, where he and his men—having increased their number from 400 to 600—entered the service of King Achish of Gath as mercenaries. Operating out of Ziklag, they raided the neighboring tribes to the southwest of the Land of Israel "all the way to Egypt" (8). David's "scorched earth" policy, "[he] left neither man nor woman alive, and took away the sheep, and the oxen, and the asses, and the camels" (9), was a nearly verbatim reprise of Saul's decimation of the priests of Nob (22:19). It is also understandable since one of the tribes attacked was Amalek, regarding whom Samuel had instructed Saul (15:3) to behave in the identical fashion (see our comments to Chapter 22).

While Achish had previously ridiculed David as "crazy" (21:16), he was apparently more than willing to prosper from David's armed forays and, as the chapter ends, Achish convinced himself that "[David] truly abhors his people, Israel, and he shall be my servant forever" (12). Stay tuned for the denouement that occurs over the course of the next two chapters.

1 Samuel 28

No, We Don't Believe in Seances, Ghosts, or the Talking Dead

A Guest Column by the Gaon R. Shmuel bar Hofni (d. 1034).

The opinion of R. Shmuel bar Hofni, Gaon of Sura, regarding the witch (*ba'alat ov*) of Endor has been known ever since it was cited by Radak (Rabbi David Kimchi) in his commentary: "He said that in spite of the fact that the Sages appear to have confirmed that the woman resurrected Samuel this cannot be accepted because it contradicts reason." Thanks to the Cairo Genizah, however, we now possess a portion of the original commentary, which took the form of a response (*teshuvah*) to a questioner. Here are some key excerpts (translated from the Judeo-Arabic).

The first question [derives] from the language of Scripture: "Saul knew that it was Samuel" (14). The Gaon's petitioner asked: If Samuel did not truly arise and was not visible, what apparition was [Saul] shown that is referred to by Scripture as "He knew"? [The Gaon] replied: Knowledge is used metaphorically to signify thought, as in "'Onan knew" (Gen. 38:9). Similarly, "Saul knew" [means] he thought, felt, and believed.

The second question: "Saul said to Samuel, 'Why have you agitated me'? And he replied, 'Why do you ask me?'" (15). This states explicitly that Samuel spoke to Saul, and he could not have spoken to him unless he was alive. We say [in response] that "Samuel said" means that Mistress 'Ob said to him that Samuel is speaking to you such and such. If one were to ask, but Scripture does not [explicitly] state that the woman said that Samuel had spoken? We would respond that while this is true, reason mandates that Scripture is only speaking from the perspective of Mistress 'Ob. This is not distinct from the language of Scripture in the case of the emissaries of the king of Jericho, "They pursued [the Israelite spies] all the way to the Jordan" (Joshua 2:7) even though they were actually with Rahab [and could not have been the subjects of the pursuit]....

[The witch also] misled him into initiating this inquiry by saying, "Whom shall I raise for you?", [leading Saul] to reply, "Raise up Samuel for me" (11), and she fooled him into thinking that she had that ability. Every time we encounter the word "he said" or "he spoke," wherein it is impossible to be the speech of the one so identified, then we may say that it may be as we have explained in this episode. If it is not impossible, then we may not purge any "said" or "spoke" of its literal sense unless it contradicts reason or is [otherwise] impossible. Look at the language of Scripture, "The vine spoke" (Judges 9:13); it is as we have explained that it is inconceivable and preposterous for a vine [to speak].

1 Samuel 29

David and the Ingrates

In this brief chapter, we learn of the vicissitudes of David's mercenary service to Achish, King of Gat. While Achish was completely persuaded of David's loyalty to him, the other Philistine overlords were downright skeptical and refused to tolerate David's presence in their midst. In their rejection, we hear echoes of David's earlier triumphs, as the Philistines once again recited the refrain of the song that the Israelite women had sung: "Saul has slain in the thousands, but David in the tens of thousands" (5; cf. 18:7, and 21:12). It is curious how these words seem to have reverberated among Israel's arch enemy and how the Philistines, who emigrated from the Aegean and whose language was not a Semitic one, nevertheless managed to learn these Hebrew words. (See our comments on Chapter 18.)

This episode also illustrates another recurring theme in David's life, namely, the failure of his patrons to appreciate him. First Saul, then Nabal, and now Achish all had considerable reason to be indebted to David, but one by one their more selfish concerns overtook their gratitude. Perhaps this is why we will eventually find David at the end of his life (1 Kings 2) dictating to Solomon his last will and testament in specific terms of who remained steadfast in their loyalty to him as opposed to who returned his favors with ingratitude.

FIRST SAMUEL

1 Samuel 30

David's Military Ethics
To the Victors—All the Victors—Belong the Spoils

In this chapter, David returned to Ziklag to discover that, in his absence, Amalekite raiders had attacked the town and carried off his wives, among others, as captives. After obtaining divine assurance of success (a fixture of those days, cf. 14:37, 22:10, 23:2, 28:6), he set out in pursuit. David then discovered an Egyptian slave who was so weak that his Amalekite master had abandoned him (presumably the slave was too weak to keep up the pace of the march). David nursed this abandoned slave back to health, and the lad repaid David's kindness by agreeing to reveal the location of the Amalekites.

David successfully counterattacked and retrieved his wives and considerable spoils. A question then arose: Were the 200 men who stayed in the camp and did not actively participate in the battle entitled to a share of those spoils? The 400 active warriors* were inclined to deny them a share, but David stipulated that "as is the share of one who goes down to the battle, so shall be the share of one who tarries by the baggage; they shall share alike" (24). The equity evident in this ruling was so impressive that Scripture tells us that this practice became standard for Israelite armies "to this very day" (25).

It is also significant that David dispatched a part of those same spoils to "the elders of Judah" (26) to be distributed amongst nearby towns that—ostensibly—had suffered at the hands of the Amalekites. This might have been out of the same sense of equity or as a practical way of obtaining their good will.

*It is tempting to suggest that the 400 active warriors were those who were in David's company since he first entered Achish's service (Chapter 21), while the 200 who "tarried" joined him only after he returned to that service later (Chapter 27). It is also noteworthy that the number of Amalekites who managed to escape David is also given as 400 (17), suggesting that it is not so much an exact number as, let us say, the average size of a battalion.

1 Samuel 31

Saul Meets His End(s)

In Chapter 28, we saw that the spirit of Samuel, ostensibly conjured up by the witch of Endor (see our comments there), had warned Saul that "tomorrow, you and your sons will be with me" (19), i.e., dead at the hands of the Philistines.

The battle atop Mt. Gilboa went poorly for Israel. The troops fled, Saul's sons were killed, and he himself was mortally wounded by Philistine archers. He summoned his armor bearer and instructed him to deliver a *coup de grâce*, "lest these uncircumcised come and run me through and make a mockery of me" (4). When the bearer declined "out of fear," Saul literally fell on his own sword. R. Yosef Kara (12th century) expressed curiosity over the bearer's fear. Since the text states that upon observing Saul's death, he, too, took his life (5), he was not afraid of such retribution as might have befallen him at the hands of Saul's relatives; rather, his was the fear of God, and he declined to participate in an assisted suicide. Why someone so fearful would commit his own suicide is left unanswered.

However, a countervailing narrative of Saul's demise was later provided to David by an Amalekite—who also referred to himself as "the son of an Amalekite *ger*" (meaning either a "convert" or a "resident"; 2 Samuel 1:13)—who claimed to have found Saul still alive and complied with the king's request to be slain. Exegetes are of various opinions regarding the relative veracity of the two accounts, observing, in part, that the Amalekite might have embellished his role in the story in order to please David and in anticipation of a reward. If that was indeed the case, he failed miserably, since David took great umbrage at the *lèse majesté* and had him executed (15–16).

Thus the saga of Saul, first king of Israel, whose appointment by Samuel met with both high anticipation and grave anxiety, came to an ignominious end.

Second Samuel

Eugène Siberdt, *The Prophet Nathan Rebukes King David*

2 Samuel 1

Saul's Last Moments

Just one chapter ago, at the end of the previous book, we took note of the fact that Saul's death was reported in two contradictory fashions. Scripture's third-person narrative, recorded in the closing chapter of 1 Samuel, has Saul falling on his own sword when his armor bearer refused to assist in his suicide. Our chapter presents the report of a survivor of the battle atop Mt. Gilboa (described variously in verses 8 and 13 as an Amalekite or the son of an Amalekite convert) who claimed to have found Saul mortally wounded on his own spear and complied with the king's request to hasten his demise (9–10). Rather than reward him, as he apparently anticipated, David had him executed for the act of *lèse majesté* he had perpetrated (14–16).

Of considerable philological interest is the word *shavatz* that Saul was said to have used to describe his condition (9); it is a *hapax legomenon*, a word that appears nowhere else in the biblical canon. (In Modern Hebrew, *shavatz* means "stroke, apoplexy.") Rashi connected it with *tashbetz* (checkered), a term used to describe one of the priestly vestments, and associated it with Saul's murder of the priests of Nob.

R. Yosef Kara (12th century) admitted that it can only be understood from its context and referred us to the Aramaic Targum that translated it as a convulsion. Radak (13th century) also defined it contextually but considered it an illness suffered by the victim of a stab wound. Most intriguing is the Malbim (19th century), who identified it as death throes, explaining that Saul was anticipating a refusal, so he hastened to explain that he already was, for all intents, dead, and therefore the Amalekite need not fear any repercussions to his actions.

2 Samuel 2

All in the Family

Earlier (1 Samuel 11), the citizens of Jabesh-Gilead had been threatened by the Ammonites, and they sought a champion to fight for their cause. Saul gathered an army of 330,000 soldiers and successfully defended them. We speculated there that Saul's concern over Jabesh-Gilead may have been due to his being descended from one of their local women, who was given in forced marriage to a Benjaminite. Here we learn that that concern was repaid by Jabesh-Gilead, whose people took Saul and Jonathan's corpses down from the walls of Beisan where they had been put on display by the Philistines and brought them to a proper Jewish burial. David acknowledged their loyalty and called on them, successfully, to transfer their allegiance to him.

This call came on the background of an imminent war of succession that pitted David against Ish-Boshet, a surviving son of Saul, whose claim to the throne was supported by Abner, Saul's chief of military staff. (This is the second indication we have had that the names of biblical characters may be symbolic rather than actual: Ish-Boshet, "Man of Shame," like Nabal, "fool," do not strike me as names given at birth.)

The opposing forces met across a pool near Gibeon, and hostilities began with a limited encounter between twelve soldiers from each side—somewhat reminiscent of the one-on-one challenge between David and Goliath—that was quickly followed by an all-out battle. The familial nature of the conflict is highlighted by the verse "The three sons of Zeruiah were there—Joab, Abishai, and Asahel" (18), the last named setting out in individual pursuit of Abner, who was able to strike him "on the fifth [rib]" (near the heart) with the blunt end of his spear and kill him (23), bringing the conflict to a sudden end.

Overlooked, perhaps, in the proverbial fog of battle, is that Abner was Saul's cousin (see 1 Samuel 14:51), just as David's forces were led by Joab, who was David's nephew (Zeruiah was one of David's sisters, cf. 1 Chronicles 2:16). This is not the last that we will hear of these warring clans (see 3:1).

2 Samuel 3

Revenge Is a Dish Best Served Cold
Abner Is Murdered, and David Is Devastated

Our chapter opens with a list of David's offspring. Implicit in this list is that in a relatively short amount of time, the number of David's wives had increased dramatically from the two who accompanied him to Hebron in the previous chapter (2:2) to a total of six.

Abner, after falling out with his liege lord, Ish-Boshet, decided to go over to David, but David imposed an unanticipated condition: David wanted Saul's daughter Michal restored as his wife. We may recall that after Michal assisted David to escape Saul's clutches, Saul took her away and gave her over to one Palti ben Layish (1 Samuel 25:44), with whom she had been living in the interim. As much as we might anticipate the newly reunited couple living the proverbial "happily ever after," David and Michal were to quarrel, and the upshot will be that "Michal, daughter of Saul, did not bear a child until the day she died" (6:23).*

Abner went on to play a significant personal role in reconciling Israel—and Benjamin in particular—with David's reign. Joab, however, had not gotten over Abner's killing of Asahel (Chapter 2). When Joab learned that David had hosted Abner in Hebron and released him peacefully (23), Joab insinuated that Abner was actually on a spying mission. Using David's authority, Joab summoned Abner back and stealthily contrived to kill him, striking him "in the fifth [rib]" just as Asahel had been struck (2:23).

David was devastated; he loudly proclaimed his innocence in the plot and composed a dirge that lauded Abner for his service to the Jewish people and bemoaned the craven way he was slain. He was particularly sensitive to the fact that as a newly installed monarch, his every act was subject to intense scrutiny and that "the sons of Zeruiah are too hard for me" (39).**

* A later reference to "the five children that Michal, daughter of Saul, bore to Adriel ben Barzilay of Meholah" (21:8) is explained (by Rashi, there) as Michal raising the children of her sister Meirav.

** Whether the killing of Abner was murder, or a justifiable act of revenge, will be the subject of an inquiry we will undertake apropos of David's parting instructions to Solomon in 1 Kings 2:5.

2 Samuel 4

What Goes Around…
Another (Somewhat Gruesome) Example of David's Honoring Saul and the Monarchy

Since our introduction to David back in 1 Samuel 16, we have been able to observe the consistency of his character. He was loyal to those who took his side, antagonistic, even vindictive, towards those who opposed him, and above all else, he demanded respect for the institution he personified—the monarchy. Those who expected to curry favor with him by disparaging Saul, such as the Amalekite in Chapter 1 who told him that he had hastened his demise, ended up incurring his wrath instead.

In this chapter, we have a reprise of this tendency. Baanah and Rechab, captains in Saul's army (and, by implication of v. 2, fellow Benjaminites and, perhaps, even relatives), turned against Ish-Boshet and delivered his head—quite literally—to David, in apparent expectation of a reward. David taught them a lesson via a *kal va-chomer* (*a fortiori* reasoning): If I exacted a price from one who reported Saul's death, a matter that occurred during a pitched battle, how much more so will I punish you who have taken a life under peaceful circumstances (10–11). Not only were they executed, but they were dismembered, a gruesome act of public shaming reminiscent of Adoni Bezek who would shame his defeated opponents by cutting off their fingers and toes (Judges 1:6) and then publicly displaying their corpses, similar to the postmortem hanging of Haman and sons (Esther 9).

Finally, yet another foreshadowing occurs, as we learn about Mephi-Boshet,* son of Jonathan, who was crippled when his nurse dropped him in her haste to escape David's expected vengeance. He is of no present consequence but will reappear later in the book (Chapter 9).

---

* Arguably (like Ish-Boshet), yet another symbolic name. Indeed, according to 1 Chronicles 8:34, his name was Meriv-Ba'al ("fighter against Baal"), also symbolic but not as awkward as Mefi-Boshet.

2 Samuel 5

The Blind and the Lame:
Did They Represent Isaac the Blind, and Jacob, Who Limped? Or Something Else Entirely?

In this chapter, all of Israel came to acknowledge David's reign and, perhaps because of his broader acceptance, he decided to move his capital from Hebron, which was strictly Judean, to the more broad-based Jerusalem—then known as Jebus. As he approached the city, however, he received the following enigmatic message from its inhabitants: "You will not enter here until you remove the *'ivrim* and the *pischim*" (6). While there are various ways in which these critical words have been translated, the consensus (including, inter alia, King James and the Jewish Publication Society) is that the former are "the blind" and the latter are "the lame." Just who were these blind and lame who were ostensibly preventing David's conquest of Jebus?

Rashi (and others), following the Midrash, explained:

> [Jebus's inhabitants] were from the descendants of Abimelech [King of the Philistines]. They had two idols, one [depicting] a blind person and one [depicting] a lame person. They were made to represent Isaac [who was blind] and Jacob [who limped]. [Placed] in their mouths was the oath Abraham swore to Abimelech [to be gracious to his descendants up to four generations, Genesis 21:23–24].

Equally perplexing is David's retort: "Whosoever strikes a Jebusite and reaches the [water] pipe (*tzinor*), and the blind and lame who are despised by David, wherefore they say 'neither blind nor lame shall enter the house'" (8). Rashi, in keeping with his previous remark, identified the *tzinor* as a tower or spire, explaining that it was there that the Jebusite idols were kept, and it had to be taken first.

R. Yosef Ibn Caspi (14th century), however, took a highly original track, combining both verses to produce the following interpretation: Inside the entrance to Jebus, as to every walled city, was a pool of water that was frequented by the wretched of society, such as the blind and the lame. The Jebusites were taunting David, saying that his chances of conquering the city were as poor as they were to overcome these wretches, who, alone, could defeat him.

After the successful conquest, David solidified his rule by building a royal palace, with the assistance of Hiram, King of Tyre, whose aid would be welcomed later by Solomon in the construction of the first Temple (1 Kings 5). David also took additional wives and concubines and, although it is not specifically indicated, chances are that some or even all those marriages were politically inspired.

2 Samuel 6

Uzzah Shoulda Known…
But He Hadn't Read His Rashi

Back in 1 Samuel 7:1, we learned that the Holy Ark, which had been captured by the Philistines and returned after they were stricken with hemorrhoids, ended up in Kiryat Ye'arim, in the home of Abinadab "on the hill." There it reposed throughout the reign of Saul and into the eighth year of David's reign, which is when he set out to retrieve it and bring it to Jerusalem. It was placed on a new wagon and accompanied by Abinadab's two sons, Uzzah and Ahio, with Ahio leading the oxen and Uzzah following.

IN THE COMPANY OF PROPHETS

At some point along the way, the oxen slumped over and Uzzah instinctively reached out towards the Ark to prevent it from sliding off the back of the wagon (6). God was angered, and He struck Uzzah dead on the spot (7). Since Uzzah appeared to have acted out of concern for the Ark, why was he so cruelly punished?

To understand the talmudic answer, let us return to Joshua 4 and repeat some of our comments there:

> At the close of [Joshua 3], we left the priests immersed up to their feet in water on the eastern bank of the Jordan, waiting with the Ark while the rest of the people crossed over. When that crossing was complete, God instructed Joshua to have the priests "ascend from the Jordan" (16–17) and "as soon as the soles of the priests' feet were drawn up unto the dry ground, the waters of the Jordan returned to their place as before" (18). To which "dry ground" were the priests' feet drawn up? While logic would have it that the reference is to the west bank of the Jordan—where the rest of the nation awaited them—a talmudic Aggadah insists that the priests retreated to the eastern bank, whereupon "the Ark bore its bearers aloft and crossed."

Rashi, following this Aggadah, explained Uzzah's sin: "He should have expounded *a fortiori* (*kal va-chomer*): The Ark carried its own porters over the Jordan, is it not all the more so [that it could carry] itself?" Rashi labeled the crime a *shegagah*, meaning unintentional, perhaps implying that the severity of his punishment was also intended to serve as a deterrent to other, similar disrespectful acts, however inadvertent or mindless.

SECOND SAMUEL

2 Samuel 7

And the Lord Gave Him Ease from His Enemies All Around

The title phrase above, which appears in the lead sentence in the current chapter, innocent as it may appear, is fraught with religious significance.

> Thus would R. Yehudah say: Israel was instructed [to perform] three *mitzvot* when they entered the land [of Israel]—to appoint a king, to eradicate the seed of Amalek, and to build themselves the Chosen House [i.e., the Temple]. (*Sanhedrin* 20b)

Curiously, a literary link connects all three of these commandments: they are all accompanied by the phrase "[rest] from their enemies all around." In Deut. 12:10, it precedes "to the place in which the Lord your God shall choose to cause his name to dwell, there you shall bring all that I command you." In Deut. 25:19, it is followed by, "You shall blot out the memory of Amalek from under the sky." And in 1 Samuel 12:11, it is an integral part of Samuel's address in response to the people's demand for a king.

This phrase also makes a cameo appearance at other critical moments. It introduces Joshua's valedictory speech (23:1) as he prepared to exit from the political stage. In Judges 2:14, the recurring theme of crime, punishment, and deliverance is described as "[God] gave them over into the hands of their enemies round about." In Judges 8:34, after the death of Gideon, the people's ingratitude is expressed in terms of abandoning God "who had delivered them out of the hand of all their enemies on every side." And in 2 Chronicles 15:15, the people rejoiced in the oath administered to them by King Azariah because it indicated that God "was fond of them and gave them rest round about."

Here, it introduces David's unrequited desire to build the Temple. God withheld that privilege from him but promised that it would be accomplished by a descendant: "He shall build a house for My name, and I will establish the throne of his kingdom forever" (13). The identity of that descendant, when provided in 1 Chronicles 22:9, incorporates our telltale phrase: "Behold, a son shall be born to you who shall be a man of rest and I will give him rest from all his enemies round about; for his name shall be Solomon (*Shelomo*), and I will give peace (*shalom*) and quietness unto Israel in his days."

2 Samuel 8

Getting Roped in: Explaining a Curious Verse

Our chapter provides a list of many of David's conquests. A seemingly offhand reference to the treatment of Moab, however, begs explanation.

> And he smote Moab and measured them with the ropes [*ba-chevel*], making them to lie down on the ground. He measured two [lengths] of rope to put to death, and one full rope to keep alive. And the Moabites became servants to David, and tributaries (2).

The ropes, we may assume, were of a standard length and served as a customary instrument of measurement in those days; hence, a demarcated territory was also called a *chevel* (cf. Deut. 3:4, 13, 14). But why the measurement? Why lying down? Why did two lengths impose a death penalty? And why did all of this happen specifically to the Moabites? We can answer our questions by combining the insights of two exegetes.

Rashi would have us harken back to 1 Samuel 22:3ff., wherein David, preparing to flee from Saul, entrusted his family's safety to the King of Moab, who, by implication, reneged on his promise of protection. (Entrusting his relatives to Moabites may have made sense to David since his own great-grandmother, Ruth, was a Moabite.) Rashi wrote:

> Those measured with two ropes were killed. [This vengeance was] because they killed his father, his mother, and his brothers as it is said, "He led them before the king of Moab." We do not find that they ever left from there.

Radak observed that forcing them to lie down (rather than be measured standing) was a demonstration of their relative inferiority and a sign of contempt.

And, by implication, people who measured more than two lengths were likely to have been older than those who measured less, so it was an objective—albeit arbitrary—way of imposing a sentence on those who were more likely to have shared in the responsibility for the fate of David's relatives.

2 Samuel 9

Mutual Loyalty? Foreshadowing of Future Events

In Chapter 4, we encountered Mephi-Boshet (*née* Meriv-Baal), son of Jonathan, who became crippled when dropped by his nurse as they were fleeing from David's anticipated vengeance against the House of Saul. At that instance, we noted David's fierce loyalty to those who befriended him, such as Jonathan, and observed that the reference to a son was likely a foreshadowing of future events. Here is where they began to come to fruition—but not yet entirely.

Ziba, one of Saul's retainers, identified Mephi-Boshet to David, who summoned him to his presence. Mephi-Boshet clearly approached David in great trepidation. David, however, in keeping with that aforementioned loyalty, made him a promise: "Fear not, for I will surely show you kindness for your father Jonathan's sake. I will restore all the land of your father Saul, and you will eat bread at my table continually" (7). Ziba, who had 15 sons and 20 servants, was put in charge of the lands that David restored to Saul's grandson, while Mephi-Boshet himself remained on in Jerusalem in order to avail himself of the king's hospitality on an ongoing basis.

There is literary foreshadowing in the concluding verse, too, detailing the extent of Mephi-Boshet's disability ("he was crippled in both legs"), which was irrelevant to his status then, but recurred with significance in the continuation (Chapter 16ff.).

Stay tuned.

2 Samuel 10

Unrequited Grace to an Unspecified Favor

David attempted to be gracious to the Ammonites—in return for an undisclosed favor—but his ambassadors suffered grievous insult at their hands and war was declared, pitting Israel against the combined forces of Ammon and its ally Aram.

Joab, David's commander-in-chief, assessed the dire situation and came up with a successful strategy: he divided the command of his forces between himself and his brother Abishai. He himself took "select" forces (9) and faced off against the Arameans, while the remainder of the army faced off against Ammon (10), with the explicit understanding that should one force be overwhelmed, the other would come to its rescue (11). Joab then declared: "Be of good courage, and let us prove strong for our people and for the cities of our God, and the Lord will do that which seems good to Him" (12), which, to be candid, can be read either as a protestation of faith or of resignation.

Although Joab's choice of the select force implies that he saw Aram as the greater threat, their forces fled before him, inspiring a similar flight by the Ammonites. This enabled Abishai to enter "the city" (14), which likely is a reference to its capital, Rabbat Ammon (whose biblical name carries on today in the Jordanian capital Amman). The Arameans, fearful of David seizing this advantage to consolidate his hold over them, gathered an even larger force and met Israel in another pitched battle at Helam (somewhere between present-day Syria and Jordan) and the result was another striking victory for David and Israel.

As to that unspecified favor David was intent on repaying in the first place, the exegetes offered a Midrash that stipulates that a sole survivor of the Moabite perfidy against David's family found refuge in Ammon. While this serves to link this chapter to his harsh treatment of the Moabites in Chapter 8, since the entire matter of the tragic fate of his family (see our comments there) is hypothetical, this would be a speculation built on another speculation. Yet it seems the best explanation that has been offered.

IN THE COMPANY OF PROPHETS

2 Samuel 11

Whoever Says David Sinned Is Mistaken:

But Stay Tuned for the Next Essay, Where We Will Claim the Opposite...

Preface: I once attended a conference on teaching Tanakh at Bar Ilan University. The subject of David and Bathsheba came up, and before the moderator could even call on her, Nehama Leibowitz was on her feet, from the audience, proclaiming: "It is prohibited to teach chapter 11, without teaching chapter 12." In deference to Nehama, I recommend reading my observations on this chapter in conjunction with the following chapter: "You are the Man... I have Sinned Against the Lord."

On the one hand, the Talmud reports the opinion of R. Shmuel bar Nahmani in the name of R. Yonatan: "Whoever says that David sinned is mistaken" (*Shabbat* 56a). On the other hand, we have the evidence of the text, which records his tryst with Bathsheba, a married woman, and his complicity in the death of her husband, Uriah, at the hands of the Ammonites. The rabbis deflected the challenge of these verses, claiming that they imply only an intent to sin, without the actual commission.

In full disclosure, the Talmud acknowledges that the impulse to exonerate David came primarily from Rabbi Yehudah HaNasi, who was descended from David and who manipulated the text (*mehapeikh ve-dareish*) to absolve him of two capital crimes—adultery and murder.

Woven together, the tapestry of the rabbinic version of the episode reads as follows: David was practicing archery when one of his arrows went astray and knocked over the screen behind which Bathsheba was bathing. Overcome by her beauty, and somehow recognizing her as the intended mother of the son who was to succeed him, he instructed Joab to send her husband, Uriah, into battle and withdraw support from him, leaving his ultimate fate, as it were, to God. As to the charge of adultery, they maintained that "whosoever went to war in David's army gave his wife a conditional divorce" so that in case a soldier died, his wife was released retroactively. Therefore, Uriah's eventual death made Bathsheba a single woman even at the time she dallied with David. (They found an absolution from the murder charge, too, but we plan to confront that when we get to 1 Kings 2.)

In contrast to the talmudic attempt to exonerate David, we have the self-evident testimony of Scripture that David, confronted by the parable of Nathan the Prophet (12:1–4), admitted his guilt (12:13) and accepted its consequences, which included the death of the infant son born of that union—although Solomon, a subsequent child by Bathsheba, did succeed him.

2 Samuel 12

"You Are the Man" "I Have Sinned Against the Lord" But Why Then Does Solomon Get to Build the Temple?

Preface: Nehama Leibowitz once claimed, "It is prohibited to teach chapter 11, without teaching chapter 12." In deference to Nehama, this post is a direct continuation of the previous chapter, "Whoever Says David Sinned Is Mistaken."

In contrast to the talmudic attempt to exonerate David, we have the self-evident testimony of Scripture that David, confronted by the parable of Nathan the Prophet (1–4), admitted his guilt (13) and accepted its consequences, which included the death of the infant son born of that union—although Solomon, a subsequent child by Bathsheba, did succeed him.

It is that confession to which Nehama alluded in her remarks about chapter 12, and her argument that David's acknowledgment of wrongdoing outweighs rabbinic attempts to find him innocent is persuasive.

But it is to Solomon that we turn here, in order to fathom how God could allow the child of an adulterous union to occupy so prominent a role in building the Temple from which David himself was precluded on account of the blood he had spilled in battle (see Chapter 7). The answer, astonishingly, is that it is precisely Solomon's checkered origin that made him the ideal candidate for that imposing task, because David had several other "skeletons" in his closet alongside which this one was content to rattle. Here, to illustrate this conclusion, is another pointed rabbinic remark.

> [God instructed Lot] "Leave the city with your wife and your two daughters who are to be *found*." R. Tobiya and R. Yitzhak said: Two *findings*, Ruth the Moabite and Naamah the Ammonite. R. Yitzhak [also] said: "I *found* My servant David" (Ps. 89:21). Where did I *find* him? In Sodom" (*Bereishit Rabbah* 41).

David, on his father's side, was descended from Ruth who—apart from the questionable nature of her liaison with Boaz—was a Moabite, and Moab was the product of the incestuous union between Lot and his elder daughter that took place right after the destruction of Sodom. Lot's younger daughter bore him Ammon (Genesis 19:37–38), who was the ancestor of Naamah the Ammonite, wife of Solomon and mother to Rehoboam, Solomon's successor (1 Kings 14:21). So the Davidic line, of which the Messiah is intended to derive, is marked all along the way by incest, adultery, and, to say the least, highly questionable and inappropriate behavior. (Recall, too, that David was descended from Judah via his dalliance with his daughter-in-law, Tamar.)

One last rabbinic adage completes the hermeneutic circle.

> R. Yohanan said in the name of R. Simeon b. Yehotzadak: One should not appoint anyone administrator of a community, unless he carries a basket of vermin on his back, so that if he became arrogant, one could tell him: Look behind you! (BT *Yoma* 22b)

2 Samuel 13

All in the Family (2)

Toward the end of our comments on the previous chapter, we noted David's descent from Judah via an affair with his daughter-in-law Tamar. This chapter leads with the tragic story of another Tamar who was subject to abuse and rape by Amnon, her half-brother, with David himself playing a crucial, albeit unwitting, role.

Tamar's degradation (verse 12 uses the word *nevalah* that we have commented on in 1 Samuel 25) unleashed a series of events that undermined the Davidic monarchy and threatened the king's very life. When David failed to react to the situation (21), Absalom, Tamar's full brother, set out to avenge his sister. Plotting over the course of two full years, he conspired to isolate Amnon at a place of his (Absalom's) choosing and had him killed. Fearing a reprisal, Absalom escaped to the land of Geshur (37) where he found sanctuary with its king, Talmay, who, recalling 2 Samuel 3:3, was his grandfather.

And yet, in the very next verse we read, "So Absalom fled, and went to Geshur, and was there three years." Why this repetition?

Don Yitzhak Abravanel (15–16th century) answered this question by parsing these two verses carefully, yielding the following plausible distinction. Initially, Absalom sought sanctuary with his grandfather, Talmay, "king of Geshur," in an undisclosed location. When the nature of David's ongoing grief ("he mourned his son daily") reached him, he feared retribution and moved to Geshur, the capital of the kingdom and, arguably, a fortified city.

The closing verse begs interpretation, too. Translated literally, it states: "And King David, she longed for Absalom; for he was comforted concerning Amnon, seeing he was dead" (39). The problem is that David, of course, is a masculine noun, while the verb "longed" (*va-tekhal*) is feminine. Rashi resolved this grammatical problem by treating the verse as elliptical (i.e., a key word is absent from the text, but implicit), saying: "David's soul [*nefesh*, feminine in Hebrew] longed." In fact, the very word "soul" is interpolated into the English translations of King James and the Jewish Publication Society (inter alia).

2 Samuel 14

Joab's Plot to Achieve Reconciliation:
The End of One Saga, the Beginning of Another

General Joab, concerned on account of David's pining away for Absalom, sought to reconcile them. Somehow skeptical of his own powers of persuasion, he hired a stand-in, "a wise woman" of Tekoa (2), a place in Judea between Jerusalem and Hebron, and scripted her role. She was to appear as a woman in protracted mourning and seek David's intervention to spare the life of her sole surviving son, who had murdered his brother and was now the object of the family's blood vengeance. Speaking quite poetically (her words or Joab's?) she said, "Thus they would quench the last ember remaining to me" (7).

David swore to her that "nary a hair [on his head] will fall to the ground" (11), but the woman requested—and received—his permission to continue, and after uttering yet another particularly poignant phrase ("For we must all die, and we are as water spilt on the ground, which cannot be gathered up again," 14), David's suspicions were raised and she admitted to him that "your servant Joab instructed me and put all these words in my mouth" (19).

David then ordered Joab to retrieve Absalom from Geshur to Jerusalem, but with the proviso that he would remain at home and never see the king (24), to which Absalom consented. After the passage of some two years, however, Absalom grew impatient, and he forced Joab into interceding on his behalf. Joab acceded, and the chapter ends with Absalom prostrating himself before David and David kissing his wayward son.

Rather than this marking the conclusion of the previous episode, it sets the next one in motion, incorporating yet another literary foreshadowing: The reference to Absalom's luxuriant hair (26) will reprise itself in an unanticipated fashion (see 2 Samuel 18:9).

2 Samuel 15

Plots and Counterplots:
Absalom Rebels, but David
Responds with a Page from His Playbook

Absalom, not content with his reconciliation with David, began to practice demagoguery and politicking by presenting himself as a potentially more favorable ruler than his father. His striking appearance (recall 14:25: "There was none in Israel as handsome as Absalom") combined with his sense of public displeasure over his father's austere rule, made a favorable impression on visitors to Jerusalem, and "he stole the hearts of the men of Israel" (6).

At a particular time designated "after forty years" (7; the exegetes regard it as the fortieth year since the initiation of the monarchy under Saul, a point at which Absalom may have thought that David had outlived his royal usefulness), Absalom, who had already demonstrated an aptitude for conspiracy (see Chapter 13), asked and received permission to relocate to Hebron, where he successfully launched a rebellion against his father with the motto "Absalom rules in Hebron" (10). Surely it was not lost on him that Hebron was both the capital of his tribe, Judah, as well as the place from which his father, in defiance of Saul, had launched his own kingdom.

David appreciated the lethal threat Absalom posed not only to his reign but to his person and promptly took flight, taking exaggerated care to be accompanied by those who could be useful to him in exile and not to encumber himself with those who could provide no practical service. (Ironically, he left behind ten of his concubines, whose taking by Absalom epitomized the latter's utter disdain for his father and could be seen as "payback" to David for his taking of Bathsheba.) He also took a page, as it were, from Absalom's playbook, leaving behind a potential fifth column in the persons of the priests, Zadok and Abiathar, whom he charged with collecting intelligence on his opponents and dispatching it to him via their sons, Ahimaaz and Jonathan, and Hushai, the "first friend" (*rei'eh David*, 37), who was specifically charged with thwarting the counsel of Ahithophel of Gilo, a particularly shrewd nemesis (and, according to a medieval Jewish folk tradition, the teacher of Socrates).

As the prophet Isaiah was later to remark: "I reared children and brought them up—And they have rebelled against Me!" (Isaiah 1:2).

SECOND SAMUEL

2 Samuel 16

Beware of Ziba Bearing Gifts and Shimei Bearing Curses

David's hasty departure from Jerusalem in the previous chapter meant that he and his household had fled on foot and without the provisions necessary to sustain them, surely not the best way to avoid capture by Absalom's rebel forces. To his aid came Ziba, servant to Saul and major domo to Mephi-Boshet, sole surviving son of Jonathan, whom we first met in Chapter 4 and again in Chapter 9. The chickens of foreshadowing are coming home to roost.

Ziba brought along donkeys for transportation, food and drink for the wayfarers, and spun a tale of conspiracy against David featuring his own master, Mephi-Boshet. If Ziba were to be believed, that son of Jonathan had set a new record for ingratitude: ignoring all that David had done for him on account of his relationship with Jonathan, his father, Mephi-Boshet had used the turmoil surrounding Absalom's rebellion to pursue the restoration of his ancestral rule. David responded by decreeing that all Mephi-Boshet's property now belonged to Ziba. When we reach the denouement of the Absalom episode, we will witness David doing a "flip flop." Caught between the rock of the solemnity with which royal decrees deserve to be met and the hard place of the discovery that Ziba had lied about Mephi-Boshet's true feelings towards him, David declared that "he and Ziba should divide the property" (19:30).

As though this were not enough of a blow to David's pride, no sooner had Ziba gone than Shimei son of Gera, another relative of Saul, seized the opportunity to heap curses upon him, jeering, "Keep going, you bloody wicked man" (7). Here, David showed remarkable restraint, accepting these taunts as part of his divinely ordained suffering, and forbidding Abishai son of Zeruiah from striking Shimei. En passant, we recall that David had earlier exclaimed "the Zeruiah boys are just too tough [or savage] for me" (2 Samuel 3:39), hinting at yet another score that will not be settled until we get to David's last will and testament (1 Kings 2).

2 Samuel 17

Plot, Counterplot, and More "I Spy"

Just as There Were Benjaminites, Relatives of Saul, Who Took David's Side, There Were Judeans, Relatives of David, Who Sided with Absalom

We recall that David had instructed his counselor Hushai to remain in Jerusalem and serve as a "fifth column" by thwarting the advice of Ahithophel (15:34). In this chapter, both of David's assumptions were validated: Ahithophel indeed delivered sage and pertinent advice to Absalom, and only Hushai was able to countermand that advice. The result was salvific for David, who lived to fight another day (22), but catastrophic for Ahithophel, who took it so personally that he returned home to Gilo and committed suicide (23). (Gilo, the southern suburb of modern Jerusalem, is situated in reasonable proximity to the biblical site of the same name.)

Yet another of David's preemptive strategies paid off in this chapter. Ahimaaz and Jonathan, sons of the priests Zadok and Abiathar, were his spies in Absalom's camp and brought him word of Hushai's success and Ahithophel's comeuppance. Some details of their escapade, however, warrant further investigation. First of all, there is the manner in which they evaded detection by Absalom's soldiers: While they hid in a well, a woman covered its mouth with drying pitas and pointed the pursuers in the wrong direction, strikingly reminiscent of the manner in which Joshua's spies were aided by Rahab (Joshua 2).

More subtle, albeit more significant, is the fact that this took place in Bahurim, which was home to Shimei son of Gera, identified as "from Saul's family" (16:5). In other words, even in a Benjaminite town populated by relatives and retainers of Saul (see also 3:16), there were those who would put themselves at risk to aid David.

On the other hand, our chapter ends with the notice that "Absalom had appointed Amasa army commander in place of Joab; Amasa was the son of a man named Ithra the Israelite, who had married Abigail, daughter of Nahash and sister of Joab's mother Zeruiah" (25). In other words, just as there were Benjaminites, even relatives of Saul (like Mephi-Boshet) who took David's side, there were Judeans, even relatives of David, who sided with Absalom. Recall that Zeruiah was one of David's sisters (cf. 1 Chronicles 2:16) and Joab was his nephew (see our comments to Chapter 2), and yet Amasa took up arms with Absalom.

2 Samuel 18

"The Forest Devoured More than the Sword" But Not a Hair of His Fell to the Ground...

The denouement of Absalom's rebellion was at hand. David divided his forces among his three commanders: the stalwart Joab, Joab's brother Avishay, and a newcomer named Ittay the Gittite, intimating that he either ran a wine press—*gat*—or was a mercenary from the Philistine city of that name. (Recall that Uriah, erstwhile husband of Bathsheba who was employed by David as a soldier, was a Hittite, and many of the 400 mercenaries who accompanied David in 1 Samuel 25:13 were probably non-Israelites, too.) Before dispatching them to the field of battle, David publicly instructed them to "go easy" on Absalom (5).

The battle took place in the Ephraim forest, and 20,000 of Absalom's soldiers were killed in what the text calls a *magefah* (7), the customary word for plague or pestilence, which, as a derivative of the verb N-G-P (to gore, as an ox), may also signify a slaughter. A postscript, however, notes—hence, the title of this commentary—"The forest devoured more than the sword" (8).

Rashi, following the venerable Aramaic version (Targum) of Yonatan ben Uzziel, interpreted this to mean "the wild animals of the forest." Radak, however, offered an alternative explanation; namely, that "they were scattered about in their flight and wounded by the trees of the forest." I believe that if we read just a bit further, we can determine which of the two interpretations is more consistent with the context.

Absalom, astride a donkey, rode beneath a tree, and his hair got entangled in a branch, leaving him suspended "between heaven and earth" (9). (Recall 14:26, an earlier foreshadowing concerning his luxuriant hair.) Joab, in direct disobedience to David's earlier instruction, stabbed Absalom three times in the heart, and ten of his armor bearers finished him off (15). There is a very subtle reminiscence here as well. In response to the wise woman of Tekoa's plea for her ostensible son, David had sworn "lest one hair of his head fall to the ground" (14:11). The fictitious son, of course, represented Absalom, who now died without his hair falling to the ground.

Considering this, Radak's interpretation that the soldiers were felled by the trees themselves appears to be more consistent with the context than Rashi's suggestion that they were killed by wild animals.

SECOND SAMUEL

2 Samuel 19

"You and Ziba Shall Split the Property"
The Sages Redress David's Inequities

With the battle over and Absalom dead, David was restored to his throne uncontested, although he did pause along the way for a bout of mourning over Absalom for which he was (properly?) rebuked by Joab. This particular incident inspired, inter alia, a late 18th-century opera, *David and Absalom*, by Bertoni, a novel, *Absalom, Absalom!*, by William Faulkner, and a madrigal, "When David Heard," by the 16th-century English composer Thomas Weelkes (still in vogue and performed by Kol Ram at a recent North American Jewish Choral Festival).

On his way back to Jerusalem, David got to replay some of the incidents that accompanied his earlier departure from that city. Shimei ben Gera apologized for hurling imprecations at him, and David excused him—to the consternation of the Zeruiah brothers. In addition, Mephi-Boshet, Jonathan's sole surviving son, revealed to him that Ziba, his servant, had lied about his disloyalty to David, forcing David to reconsider his earlier edict awarding Mephi-Boshet's property to Ziba (16:4). However, instead of entirely revoking it, David equivocated, ruling that "you and Ziba shall split the property" (30).

Both these actions by David drew rabbinic attention due to their failure to conform to the norms of equity. Shimei, as argued by Avishay (22), was a despicable traitor for cursing David and clearly warranted execution. Ziba was guilty of lying to the king even if he assisted his flight rather than hinder it; he certainly did not deserve to be rewarded by retaining his ill-gotten gains. Rabbinic traditions attempt to resolve both issues.

According to the Talmud (*Megillah* 12b-13a), Shimei was left alive because he would turn out to be an ancestor of Mordechai, thereby allowing divine retribution to take its course when his descendant saw to the execution of Haman whose own ancestor, Agag, King of Amalek, was egregiously spared by King Saul (see 1 Samuel 15)—to whom Shimei was related. And as for the inequitable division of property between Ziba and Mephi-Boshet, a Midrash (cited by Radak) states that it caused a heavenly voice (*bat kol*) to announce the eventual division of David's kingdom amongst Rehoboam, his grandson, and Jeroboam ben Nebat, who usurped it.

2 Samuel 20

Rebellion — Take 2

It Is Forbidden to Hand Over Individuals to the Enemy – Unless It Is a Criminal Like Sheba Ben Bichri

The previous chapter ended on the sour note of an argument between the "men of Israel" and the "men of Judah" over whose loyalty to David was greater, an indication that while he had been victorious over Absalom, he had not entirely eliminated the sources of discontent within his kingdom. It is, therefore, not surprising that our chapter opens with an incipient rebellion led by a "worthless" (*b'li-ya'al*) Benjaminite man named Sheba ben Bichri. David assigned the task of recruiting an army to Amasa ben Yether—who, along with Joab and Abishai, had led his forces against Absalom. Inexplicably, Amasa failed to abide by David's timetable, and it was left to Joab and Abishai to take the battle to the enemy. When Amasa finally made an appearance, Joab contrived to kill him, and his body was dumped unceremoniously along the side of the road.

The rebels eventually took refuge in a place called Abel of Beth-Maacah, which was then besieged by Joab and in imminent danger of being conquered, when a wise woman spoke up. Addressing Joab directly, she challenged his willingness to inflict such extensive collateral damage by destroying an entire city and its population and proposed surrendering Sheba in return for its safety. They struck a deal, and Sheba's head was cast down from the city ramparts, ending the siege.

The role this incident plays in the talmudic discussion of the laws of *piku'ah nefesh*—saving lives—is of considerable significance. The question (JT *Terumot* 8) was raised how to respond if non-Jewish brigands say that if one Jew is surrendered to them, they will allow the others to go free, or else they will kill them all. While the law is that they must all face death rather than surrender one of their own, an exception was made for someone who, like Sheba ben Bichri, was guilty of a capital crime (in his case, treason) and, arguably, had already forfeited his life.

2 Samuel 21

Beware the Polydactyl!
(Not to Be confused with a Pterodactyl!)

And Three Other Giants, Ishbi Benob, Saph, and None Other Than Goliath Jr.

The second half of this chapter (15–22) describes the encounters between David's forces and four truly outstanding Philistine opponents: the children of Rafah. Assuming that R-P-H is identical with R-P-', these are four of the race of giants (the Septuagint translates Refa'im as either *gigantes* or *titanon*) that we have already encountered on a number of previous occasions, ranging from Og King of Bashan to Goliath of Gat. Let us look at each of the four escapades.

In the first (16–17), Ishbi Benob, "whose spear was three hundred shekels of brass in weight," was taken down by the combined efforts of David and Avishai. Second, a giant named Saph was slain by a warrior named Sibkhai of Hushat. Third, Goliath the Gittite (likely named for the earlier Philistine hero to whom, by virtue of his size, he was probably related), "the staff of whose spear was like a weaver's beam," was slain by a Bethlehemite named Elchanan whose father's name is given as Ya'rei Orgim, which can fairly be translated into Hebrew as a weaver's (*orgim*) beam (*ya'ar* = forest → tree → beam).

The fourth matchup, featured in the title of these remarks, pitted David's own nephew Yehonatan against an anonymous giant of whom we have but a key physical description: "He had six fingers on every hand, and six toes on every foot, twenty-four [digits] in number" (20). Poly (many) dactyly (finger—related to digital) is a congenital variance that occurs in 1 of every 3,000 births and can be resolved through surgery. One assumes that in this case it added to the fearsome appearance of the otherwise anonymous giant.

Without treating additional specifics, there is, nevertheless, a significant overall observation to be made here; namely, the mere fact that there were four such giants. As we have noted previously (see our comments to Joshua 14 and 15), Hebron was also known as Kiryat Arba because it was settled (originally?) by four giants named Anaq, Achiman, Sheishai, and Talmai. Either giants come naturally in groups of four (there were 12 Titans, who could have been grouped by fours), or it is just a coincidence. Take your pick.

SECOND SAMUEL

2 Samuel 22

David's Valedictory: A Poetic Analysis

Rich Hebrew Terms Deepen Our Understanding of the Stark Imagery Employed

Here, we have, in classic biblical poetic form, David's own retrospective on his forty-year reign, composed, as the opening verse indicates, "on the day that God had delivered him from the hands of Saul and all his [other] enemies." From a textual perspective, we should note that the poem repeats itself, essentially, in the form of Psalm 18. Indeed, well-known to many is the appearance of the final verse—#51 in both texts—in the Grace after Meals, wherein the alternation between two versions of M-G-D-L (*magdil/migdol*) is assigned to weekdays versus Sabbaths and festivals.

In previous texts (specifically Exodus 14–15, Judges 4–5), we have seen narrative accounts alongside poems and acknowledged that comparisons between the two would be productive. In the present case, however, a comparison would be constrained by the sheer size of the narrative that would have to be contrasted—the entire book we call 2 Samuel and a goodly portion of its predecessor, too—all of which fit the aforementioned qualification of deliverance from both Saul and other enemies. That said, we can still focus on a few aspects.

I would like to look at verses 5–6, following the old (1917) Jewish Publication Society translation: "For the waves of Death compassed me. The floods of Belial assailed me. The cords of Sheol surrounded me. The snares of Death confronted me." In condensed paraphrase, David was saying: "I was in mortal danger," comparing the threats to his life, first, to being engulfed by water and, second, to being ensnared in a trap.

A closer reading, however, makes several finer distinctions possible.

- David spoke of *mishbarim*, from the verb SH-B-R, "to break," signifying breakers rather than more ordinary "waves" (*galim*).
- Note the unusual verb he used for what the translators rendered as "compassed," namely, *afafuni*. If we relate it to the noun *af*, meaning "nose," we may obtain the impression that David was saying—essentially—that the hazardous waters had reached his nose and that he was in imminent danger of drowning in them.
- Sheol, the netherworld, is possessed of ropes ("cords," *chavalim*), and its poetic synonym Death (*mavet*) is characterized by traps/snares (*mokshim*, Modern Hebrew for landmines), indicating that they lie in wait, so to speak, for the unwary.
- While the ropes encircled him, the snares "confronted" him (*kidmuni*, from the preposition *kodem*, meaning "in front of"). However, it can be related, etymologically, to the word for the "shinbone" (Arabic: *kadam*, the forepart of the leg), suggesting that David was nearly "cut off at the knees."

2 Samuel 23

David's Other Valedictory: A Close Reading

Highly Lyrical, and Highly Cryptic…

Our chapter opens with a highly lyrical, and highly cryptic, valedictory. We will try—as we did in the previous chapter—to extract its significance by focusing on the language. Here is the text (1–7) according to the 1917 Jewish Publication Society translation:

- "Now these are the last words of David... the anointed [*mashiach*] of the God of Jacob, And the sweet singer of Israel."
  Note that the title *mashiach* means "anointed" and neither savior nor deliverer. Recalling that David's first public appearance was as Saul's harpist, we are not surprised that he was called a sweet singer. That is also consistent with his prominence throughout the Book of Psalms.
- "The spirit of the Lord spoke by me, and His word was upon my tongue."
  Taken strictly literally, this would indicate that David was a prophet, a position adopted, for example, by Se`adyah Gaon (10th century) in the context of assigning him the exclusive authorship of Psalms.
- "Ruler over men shall be the righteous, even he that ruleth in the fear of God."
  David acknowledged that while he ruled by "divine right," that imposed on him obligations of justice and morality rather than freeing him to act arbitrarily.
- "And as the light of the morning, when the sun riseth, A morning without clouds; When through clear shining after rain, The tender grass springeth out of the earth."
  The imagery here appears to be standard poetic; i.e., there is nothing about it either overtly theological in general, or even Jewish in particular.
- "For an everlasting covenant (*b'rit olam*) He hath made with me..."
  The phrase *b'rit olam*, which appears 12 times in Tanakh, translated here as "everlasting covenant," can also mean "covenant of yore." In that latter sense, it may allude to the belief that the

Davidic dynasty was destined to rule over Israel and that Saul's ascent to the throne was inevitably temporary.

- "But the ungodly, they are as thorns thrust away, all of them, for they cannot be taken with the hand."

  The "ungodly" (or, as we prefer, worthless—see chapter 20) are compared to thorns (cf. Jer. 17:6); their prickly nature suggests that we avoid them.

- "... and they shall be utterly burned with fire in their place."

  The combination of evildoers and burning thorn bushes recalls Psalm 118:12: "They compass me about like bees; they are quenched as the fire of thorns; verily, in the name of the Lord I will cut them off."

In sum, it will take great strength to eradicate evil, but God will empower a righteous leader to accomplish this.

2 Samuel 24

A Senseless Census and a Problem of Theodicy: A Challenge for Readers through the Ages

In this chapter, David commissioned a census and suffered its consequences. One verse and one moral are of singular note.

Verse 14 is noteworthy because it is the liturgical introduction to Psalm 6, which is the quintessential prayer of supplication (*tachanun*) over whose recitation (or, more commonly, omission) daily worshippers are wont to good-naturedly argue. The noteworthy moral relates to the reason for which David was supplicating to the Lord, i.e., to ameliorate the consequences of the census he had conducted. The Torah seems to anticipate the need to conduct a census and stipulates, "Whenever you do a per capita census of the Children of Israel, let each of them pay a poll tax of half a shekel to the Lord in lieu of a head count, lest a plague break out on account of the head count" (Exodus 30:12). Indeed, it seems to be such a mundane matter that Rashi, here, expressed his perplexity over its lethal outcome, saying "I do not know what they did [wrong]."

In many respects, this situation is reminiscent of one we encountered in chapter 21. There, we read how God brought a multi-year famine on Israel on account of a wrong that Saul had perpetrated against the Gibeonites, and how David sought to rectify the situation by handing over seven of Saul's descendants for execution. Here, too, the Torah seems to say its piece unequivocally, "Children shall not be put to death on account [of the crimes] of their parents" (Deut. 24:16). In both cases, then, we confront the challenge philosophers and theologians call theodicy, God's administration of justice in the face of evil, which becomes particularly trenchant here when we consider the stipulation that "God incited David, saying go count the people" (1).

The medieval exegetes were also alert to this and offered the following explanation. It is permissible to conduct a census for a constructive purpose; it is prohibited to do so for no good reason—and David had no good reason. Therefore, it would appear that the only objective he could have had was to satisfy his own need for self-gratification ("look at how many people I rule over!") and that incurred a penalty for both him and for those who willingly participated in it.

But if you are still troubled by the problem of vicarious punishment, you are in the company of Rashi, and how bad can that be?

Samuel in Retrospect; Kings in Prospect

The Book (in two parts) of Samuel starts with an incipient monarchy (see our comments to 1 Samuel 2: "Hannah's Prayer and Kingship") and concludes with an incipient dynasty. In between, we encountered Samuel, the first "apostolic" prophet (see our further comments on 2 Kings 5), Saul, the first king, and the vicissitudes of his relationship with David, his successor, and the vicissitudes of David's relationships with his wives and sons, particularly Absalom.

Small wonder, then, that the Book (also in two parts) of Kings leads with the continuation of intramural strife as David's sons Adonijah and Solomon struggle for his throne. The role played by Batsheva in securing Solomon's throne is reminiscent of Hannah's involvement on behalf of Samuel, and the intercession of the prophet Nathan on Bathsheba's behalf should be seen in the light of his earlier remonstrations with David over her (2 Samuel 12).

The subsequent division of the unified Davidic and Solomonic kingdom into the separate northern (Ephraim) and southern (Judean) kingdoms likewise resonates with earlier internal conflict such as that exhibited during the tenure of Jephthah (Judges 12), which also featured a discordant Ephraim. That Saul was of the tribe of Benjamin; that Jeroboam ben Nebat, who was to inaugurate the breakaway kingdom (1 Kings 11), was also an Ephraimite; indicate that the dissension that was rife among the twelve sons of Jacob over the status of the children of Leah versus those of Rachel lived on.

Small wonder, again, that one of the most poignant prophetic prognoses of consolation features the reunification of the two kingdoms, Judah and Joseph/Ephraim, under the unified rule of a Davidic monarch (e.g., Ezekiel 37:15ff.), and that the Sages' forecast for the eschatological future added a Messiah ben Joseph as a precursor to the better-known Messiah ben David.

First Kings

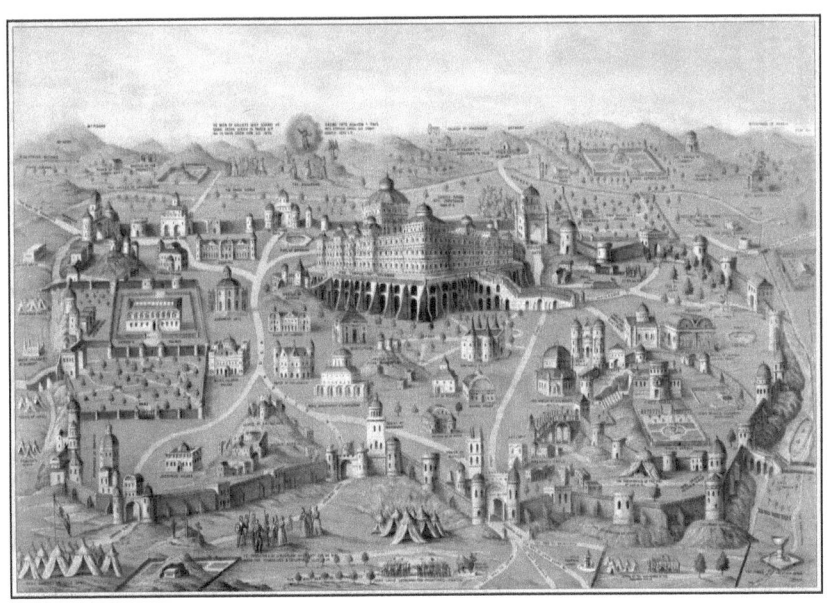

The ancient city of Jerusalem with Solomon's Temple (c. 1871)

1 Kings 1

A Look Ahead at What's in Store:
The Seeds of Dissolution Are Already Planted

The Book of Samuel gave us insight into the introduction to the idea of monarchy, which was sought, initially (harken back to 1 Samuel 8), as an antidote to the weakness of tribal leadership that characterized the earlier era of the Book of Judges. Now, with our entry into the Book of Kings, we will witness how that institution fared after the death of its dynastic founder, David, until its discontinuation at the time of the destruction of the Temple of Solomon by the Babylonians in 586 BCE—an era of over 400 years.

Caveat lector—a word of caution to the reader. At some point in the first half of the Book of Kings, the kingdom will split in two: the "Ten Tribes" led by Ephraim and known as the Kingdom of Israel, and the Kingdom of Judah, which also included Benjamin. Hence, the title "King of Israel" will no longer identify a member of the Davidic dynasty but any of a series of rulers who will command the breakaway kingdom.

The scene for the eventual dissolution of David's kingdom is set in the first chapter, as he is shown to be enfeebled by advancing age to such an extent that he failed to recognize an incipient plot to usurp his throne. The erstwhile usurper was Adonijah ben Hagit "who was born after Absalom" (6), a neat double-entendre, as he followed him in the birth line (see 2 Samuel 3:3–4) as well as in his opposition to their father's will. As if that were not enough of a coincidence, we are further notified that they were both handsome. David had a soft spot for Adonijah, too, and was unable to remonstrate with him over his behavior (6).

On this occasion, however, there were other forces at work in the palace, and sides were quickly drawn up: Joab (military) and Abiathar (priesthood) side with Adonijah, while, correspondingly, Zadok (priesthood) and Benayahu (military) side with…? As of then, they have no side to take, so all we can be told is that "they did not side with Adonijah" (8). To redress that situation, Nathan the Prophet (prominent in 2 Samuel 7 and 12) colluded with Bathsheba to successfully ensure that David's choice of Solomon as his successor would be preserved.

A literary note: Word of Solomon's succession was brought to Adonijah by Jonathan ben Abiathar who was welcomed as "a messenger of good news" (42). This is the very same Jonathan who carried intelligence to David about Absalom (2 Samuel 17), supporting our earlier observation about the reprise of Absalom's rebellion in Adonijah's attempted usurpation. It also illustrates the fickleness of loyalties when they are put to the test.

1 Kings 2

"One Cannot Delegate the Commission of a Crime" —

The Murder Charge Doesn't Stick, but Solomon Got Joab for Treason

We have already alluded to the events in this chapter on previous occasions. In 2 Samuel 3, we noted that we would revisit here the question of whether Joab's killing of Abner was justifiable as an act of blood vengeance, or if it was coldblooded murder. In 2 Samuel 11–12, we indicated that at that same revisiting, we would address the question of David's killing of Uriah. These ingredients come together in the following talmudic Aggadah (legend):

FIRST KINGS

> [King Solomon] brought Joab to trial and said to him: Why did you kill Abner? He replied: I was avenging [my brother] Asael. Was Asael not in pursuit of Abner? ... Since Abner was able to strike him at the fifth rib... he could have just wounded him.
>
> [Solomon] said: Why did you kill Amasa? [Joab] replied: Because Amasa committed treason against the king. "The king [David] ordered Amasa to summon all the men of Judah in three days' time... Amasa went to summon them and tarried" (2 Samuel 20:4ff.) ...
>
> [So why was Joab executed?] He was a traitor, as it states: "The news reached Joab who had sided with Adonijah, although not with Absalom" (1 Kings 2:28). (*Sanhedrin* 49a)

The conclusion appears to be that while Joab was morally guilty regarding Abner and Amasa, he was not legally culpable. The passage continues:

> God brought [Joab's] guilt down upon his own head for having struck down two more righteous and better men than he [Abner and Amasa]. Better, in that they construed the "buts and onlys" [see our comments on Joshua 1], while he did not, and more righteous, in that they refused a command [from Saul, to slay the priests of Nob] that came [only] orally, while he obeyed a command [to place Uriah in jeopardy] that came in writing.

That last reference addresses the question of David's guilt or responsibility for the death of Uriah. Since his order to Joab ("in writing") was plainly illegal, Joab should have refused to obey it. Indeed, by following it, he exposed himself to its consequences, pursuant to the talmudic stipulation:

> If one commissions an agent to commit murder and he complies, the agent is guilty, but the principal is exempt. Shammai the Elder said in the name of the prophet Haggai, the principal [too?] is guilty, as it states [of David]: "You slew Uriah… by the sword… and killed him by the Ammonite sword" (2 Samuel 12:9; *Kiddushin* 43a).

David's guilt, notwithstanding the above exclusion, is explained by Radak (2 Samuel 12:9):

> Generally, a person should refrain from following the king's orders in such a case. We have explained, apropos of "Anyone who defies your word shall die" (Joshua 1:18), that this does not include the commission of a crime, as the verse states: "*Only*" [be firm and resolute, excluding instructions that violate Torah law]. Not everyone, however, is capable of construing "buts" and "onlys." The onus [punishment], therefore, is on the king.

1 Kings 3

Solomon Got More Than He Bargained For

Having settled his father's scores, Solomon set out to consolidate his own kingdom. Beginning with his nearest neighbor, Egypt, he married Pharaoh's daughter. He then set about building his palace, a multi-year venture, and, in the absence of a temple, took advantage of a loophole in the law that allowed for sacrifices to be offered on a platform, or shrine (*bamah*), the largest of which, at this point in time, was situated in Gibeon.

FIRST KINGS

This marks the debut of a trope that will recur throughout the Book of Kings: A king will be acknowledged for all his meritorious deeds, but a caveat will follow to the effect that "however, the platforms were not removed; the people continued offering sacrifices and incense on the platforms."

It was in Gibeon and on the occasion of a massive sacrifice that God appeared to Solomon in a dream and offered him whatever he would wish for. Read verses 11–14 closely, and you should notice an internal inconsistency. Did you catch it? God mentioned three things for which Solomon could have asked but did not: long life, riches, and victory over his enemies. Instead, he asked for wisdom to judge the people (10). God told Solomon that He would grant him his wish, adding: "I also grant you what you did not ask for." However, while the riches and glory seem to be unconditional, the long life is made conditional on his "observing the commandments."

Radak, our stalwart *peshat* commentator on the Early Prophets, noted the contradiction and, based upon Deut. 17:12, "and lest [the king] stray from the commandments right or left in order to extend his rule over his kingdom for many years," he explained:

> This, indeed, came to pass. Because he failed to observe God's commandments, he did not live long, only 52 years. However, he possessed wealth and glory throughout his life.

Another medieval commentary, attributed to Rashi's disciple Yosef Kara, draws our attention to the fact that Solomon acquired wealth and glory as a direct consequence of his wisdom, to wit: "Throughout the land, they sought to see Solomon and to hear the wisdom God had implanted in his heart. Each would bring a gift of silver and gold…" (1 Kings 10:24–5).

IN THE COMPANY OF PROPHETS

1 Kings 4

Parsing the Royal Entourage

Then, as Now, Taxes Are a Central Feature of Government Policy

This chapter begins with a pithy statement: "King Solomon was now king over all Israel" (1) and concludes with hyperbole: "Judah and Israel were as numerous as sands of the sea; they ate and drank and were content" (20). In between, it proceeds to enumerate the members of Solomon's retinue, presenting some surprises and several questions.

First, verse 3 names two people who served as scribes (*sof'rim*) and one who was a recorder (*mazkir*). What, exactly, were their functions? Rashi identified the former as the court chroniclers and the latter as a registrar who insured that the king dealt with the cases that came before him in their proper sequential order.

Verse 2 names Azariah son of Zadok as "the priest," while verse 4 names Zadok and Abiathar as priests (*kohanim*). This raises two questions: (1) we know that Zadok had a son named Ahimaaz (who carried messages for the Davidic underground in 2 Samuel 17), but who is Azariah? And (2) how could Abiathar serve as a *kohen* when we were told earlier that Solomon dismissed him (2:27)? Radak identified Azariah as the son of Ahimaaz and, therefore, Zadok's grandson, since it is not unusual for biblical genealogies to conflate the two. He also suggested that this Zadok cannot be the one who was dismissed by Solomon, but "another priest with the same name." In fact, the register of high priests in 1 Chronicles 5 indicates that from the inception of the First Temple until its destruction (spanning some ten generations), Zadok (or, Jehozadak), Ahitub, and Azariah account for half of the names.

Verse 5 names "the king's companion," a title we encountered previously as belonging to Hushai, who served David in that capacity (2 Samuel 15:37). Radak defined the position as "he was with him constantly," and, perhaps, in contemporary terms, he would be designated "the first friend." And finally, verse 6 identifies Adoniram who was "in charge of the *mas*," which refers to the levy in the form of military service that Solomon imposed on all Israel (5:27–28) and which was to be a prime cause in the splitting of the kingdom after his death (Chapter 12).

1 Kings 5

The Details of Solomon's Rule

This chapter details the extent of Solomon's rule in both geographical and fiscal terms. He was unchallenged anywhere "from the river" (i.e., the Euphrates) all the way south to the Egyptian border (v.1), and he maintained a lavish and expensive lifestyle (2–3, 6ff.). The problem here is verse 4, which does not appear to add anything of substance to verse 1, which already established the sphere of his influence, save for the inclusion of the appositive phrase "from Tifsah to Gaza."

A stipulation of traditional exegesis is that nothing in the Bible is redundant or extraneous, so what are we to derive from these words?

Radak reported on a talmudic disagreement over the significance of these two place names:

> Rav and Shmuel [disagreed]. One said Tifsah was at one end of the world and Gaza was at [the other] end of the world. One said Tifsah and Gaza were adjacent to each other. Just as he ruled [uncontested] over Tifsah and Gaza, so was he able to rule over the rest of the world (*Megillah* 11a).

Another talmudic discussion pertinent to this chapter came apropos of verse 31, which describes the great stones that likely served in the foundation of the Temple as "hewn." The Rabbis saw this as an ostensible contradiction to a later verse: "No hammer or axe or any iron tool was heard in the House while it was being built" (6:7), and resolved it as follows: "They prepared them outside and brought them within" (*Sotah* 48b).

The Rabbis were as meticulous in their investigation of the text of Kings as Solomon himself was in his design and construction of the Temple.

1 Kings 6

A Comment on Chronology

> In the four hundred and eightieth year after the Israelites left the land of Egypt, in the month of Ziv—that is, the second month— in the fourth year of his reign over Israel, Solomon began to build the House of the Lord (v. 1).

Our chapter stipulates that construction on the Temple began 480 years after the Exodus. Our challenge is to see how many of those years can be accounted for by ordinary, textual, means.

First, we know with certainty that the period between the Exodus and entering the Land of Israel was 40 years. We also know that Saul ruled for 2 years, and David for 40 years, which, along with Solomon's 4, account with certitude for 86 years. It is with the intervening period, reflecting the eras of Joshua and the Judges, that we run into a problem: Even if we had a record of how many years each judge ruled, we do not know whether they were all consecutive rather than overlapping, nor do we know how long of a gap there may have been between even consecutive tenures.

We do, however, have a significant piece of chronological information, courtesy of Jephthah. The King of Ammon had raised the issue of the legitimacy of Israel's right to the land east of the Jordan, claiming that "when Israel came from Egypt, they seized the land that is mine" (Judges 11:13). In his reply, Jephthah argued that "Israel has been inhabiting [these lands] for three hundred years, why have you not tried to recover them all this time?" (26). That would close our gap to a bit less than a century, and we could assume that the outstanding time was subsumed in the period between Jephthah and the inauguration of Saul.

An alternative explanation, albeit less traditional, would stipulate that the number 480 is symbolic, or representational ("typological"). Given that a typical biblical generation lasted approximately 40 years (we have noted two such examples in our own brief accounting above), 480 could be understood as a formulaic way of saying 12 generations. In fact, if we return to the priestly genealogy of 1 Chronicles 5 that we cited in chapter 4, and we count backwards from Azariah "who was the priest in the House that Solomon built" (36), we arrive at Phinehas, son of Elazar, son of Aaron, a contemporary of the Exodus. This way we have no need to account for a missing century.

1 Kings 7

The Temple and the Palace: Which Is Better: Building Slowly or Quickly?

There the thrones for judgment stood; thrones of the house of David — Psalms 122:5

By combining the first verse in this chapter with the final verse of the preceding chapter, we can arrive at two different conclusions:

1. Solomon completed the Temple in seven years, while the work on his palace took thirteen years.
2. While Solomon spent only seven years building the Temple, he spent thirteen years on his palace.

The first can be complimentary (he completed the Temple in a more efficient fashion) while the second can be derogatory (he spent more time and, implicitly, more effort, on his palace). For which option do you vote? Would it influence your vote if I told you that Rashi's commentary supports the former? He wrote: "In work of the Most High he hurried, but in his own [work] he was slow; Scripture tells this to praise him." Implicit in Rashi's commentary is the assumption that Solomon commenced both construction projects at the same time. Radak, however, argued that they were consecutive. Does that change your opinion? (See our follow-up note in chapter 9.)

On account of his wisdom (which he sought in order to prosecute justice, see 3:10), Solomon made the administration of justice a hallmark of his reign, so much so, that he set aside a room in his palace for that exclusive purpose. "He made the throne portico, where he was to pronounce judgment, the Hall of Judgment. It was paneled with cedar from floor to floor" (7). Whereas we might have expected the prepositional phrase "from wall to wall," Scripture uses the somewhat clumsier "floor to floor," which Rashi—relying on the Aramaic Targum—interpreted as "from foundation to foundation, [i.e.] from the base of this wall to the base of the other wall."

In a sense, the throne of justice room paid for itself, since, as we have already noted (in chapter 3), Solomon's reputation for wise judgment earned him both glory and wealth: "Throughout the land, they sought to see Solomon and to hear the wisdom God had implanted in his heart. Each would bring a gift of silver and gold…" (1 Kings 10:24–5).

FIRST KINGS

1 Kings 8

The Month of "Ethanim"
A Festive Time of Year for Dedicating the Temple

Solomon invited all the tribal and patriarchal leaders of Israel (1) to participate in the ceremony that marked the transfer of the Ark and other holy paraphernalia from the City of David to the newly constructed Temple. Perhaps bearing in mind the tragedy that had accompanied the Ark's earlier transfer from Kiryat Ye'arim to the home of Obed Edom the Gittite (as reported in 2 Samuel 6) when Uzzah's life was lost because he reached out to steady the Ark on its wagon, this time it appears that everything was transported personally by the appropriate priests and Levites. And whereas there is no explicit reference to fanfare, in its literal sense of blaring trumpets, the move was certainly accompanied by figurative fanfare, as they sacrificed "sheep and oxen in such abundance that they could not be numbered or counted" (5).

A linguistic curiosity, however, surrounds the date on which this auspicious move was made. It is recorded in our chapter as having taken place "at the Feast, in the month of Ethanim—that is the seventh month" (2), in other words, during Sukkot, which, as we know, occurs during the month of Tishrei. So why not just name the month?

The names by which we know the present Jewish calendar (Tishrei, Marheshvan, Kislev, etc.) are late, having "made aliyah" (*alu imahem*) from Babylonia along with the Jews who returned from captivity there (Jerusalem Talmud, *Rosh Hashanah* 1:2). Tanakh utilizes ordinal numbers for months (first, second, third, etc.), which can be problematic if you do not know when the series begins. Indeed, it would appear that prior to the Exodus, the first month was Tishrei and only thereafter did it become Nisan (see Exodus 12:2), with Tishrei falling back—as it were—into seventh place, which is when our ceremony took place.

Why was Tishrei called "Ethanim," which literally means "firm or steadfast"? Yosef Kara explained that it is because once the hot, dry summer months are over, trees and grass begin to harden. Radak stated that it is because the fruits and grains that are harvested during that month are the mainstay of our diets. Ralbag (Gersonides) thought that it is because the principal festivals occur in it, and Ibn Kaspi—inspired, perhaps, by his Provencal roots—said that it reflects the hard work that farmers put into the harvest. Last—actually first—but not least, the rabbinic interpretation identifies the Patriarchs as the "steadfast" ones and observes that they were all born in Tishrei (*Rosh Hashanah* 11a).

1 Kings 9

Solomon and the "Land for Peace" Option: A Jewish King Swaps Lands with a Foreign Ruler

Incredibly, King Solomon, who ruled approximately 3,000 years ago, got himself involved in a highly contested modern and contemporary issue: whether land that is under Jewish sovereignty can be ceded to another jurisdiction. Just as incredible is that several of our traditional exegetes were exercised over it.

> At the end of twenty years during which Solomon constructed the two buildings, the Lord's house and the royal palace—Since King Hiram of Tyre had supplied Solomon with all the cedar and cypress timber and gold that he required—King Solomon in turn gave Hiram twenty towns in the region of Galilee (10–11).

On the surface, this appears to be a benign transaction. Hiram was very helpful in securing material and specialized labor for the Temple and for the palace, and Solomon gave him the towns as a token of his gratitude. However, the question, as formulated by Malbim (19th century) is: "Is it conceivable that Solomon would give Hiram Israelite towns, thereby nullifying their sanctity, which is against Torah law?" This question was anticipated long before Malbim; indeed, Radak, Ralbag (Gersonides), and Abravanel also dealt with it.

All three treatments of this question revolved around the observation that in 2 Chronicles 8:1–2 the roles are reversed: "At the end of twenty years during which Solomon constructed the house of the Lord and his palace—Solomon also rebuilt the cities that Huram [Hiram] had given to him, and settled Israelites in them."

The medieval resolution of the dilemma was captured succinctly by Ralbag: "It is already recorded in the Book of Chronicles that Hiram, too, gave towns to Solomon in which [Solomon] settled Israelites. That was entirely proper, because it is inconceivable that a king should diminish the Land of Israel." In contemporary terms, it was a land swap. Malbim seems to suggest that the actual sequence places Kings before Chronicles and that Hiram rejected the gift and returned to Solomon the same twenty towns he had received from him so—ultimately—no harm and no foul.

1 Kings 10

The Stuff of Which Legends Are Made

Who was the Queen of Sheba? We do have some biblical clues, but the rest is pure speculation—perhaps even fantasy.

First, let us examine the biblical evidence. In really ancient times, Sheba appears to have been a reasonably popular name, occurring no fewer than three times in Genesis: first, as a son of Kush (son of Ham, son of Noah; Gen. 10:7); second, as a son of Joktan (son of Eber, son of Shem, son of Noah; Gen. 10:28); and, finally, as a son of Jokshan (son of Abraham via Keturah; Gen. 25:3). (Note: Apart from the striking similarity between the names Joktan and Jokshan, the first and third Shebas each had a brother named Dedan.) There are also three references to Sheba in Ezekiel, where Dedan is also mentioned, and the raiders who slew Job's children and looted his home are also identified with Sheba (1:15). However, since Utz, Job's homeland (and likely the source of L. Frank Baum's *Oz*), is otherwise unidentified, that's not much help.

Here is the commentary on verse 1 of Ralbag/Gersonides, who lived in Provence in the 14th century. See if you can tell where the biblical allusions end and the speculation begins:

> In the Book of Ben Sirah, it is written that she was the mother of Nebuchadnezzar. She was born to one of the sons of the concubines, whom Abraham banished from the presence of his son Isaac [Gen. 25:5], advising them to distance themselves lest they subjugate Isaac's descendants, because anyone subjugating Isaac's descendants would never ever recover. Now, when they heard that Solomon was a world ruler, they thought that he was the Messiah whom Abraham had told them to anticipate. That is why the Queen of Sheba came when "she heard of Solomon's fame through the name of the Lord," hearing that Solomon ruled the world, even over the shades and the birds.

NB: The Book of Ben Sirah to which Ralbag referred is not the apocryphal book of that name, but a work of lesser repute known as the Alphabet of Ben Sirah. Also, the legend of the Queen of Sheba features in Islam as well, which identifies her with the South Arabian kingdom of Saba' and dates the arrival there of the first Yemenite Jews to the time of Solomon. The Ethiopic Church adopted it too, claiming that the kings of Ethiopia were descended from the union of Solomon and the Queen of Sheba. Hence, the renowned Emperor Haile Selassie referred to himself as The Lion of Judah.

1 Kings 11

The Torn Cloak, Reprised
Once Again, a Kingdom Is Torn from Its King

In our comments to 1 Samuel 15, we discussed whether Samuel or Saul tore one or the other's cloak. While we decided that Saul tore Samuel's cloak inadvertently, we also considered the possibility that the tearing was deliberate. In that context, we entered into evidence verses 29–30 of the present chapter: "During that time, Jeroboam went out of Jerusalem and the prophet Ahijah of Shiloh met him on the way. He had put on a new robe; and when the two were alone in the open country, Ahijah took hold of the new robe he was wearing and tore it into twelve pieces."

Once again, we have one robe, two parties, and four possibilities, since each party might have torn his own robe or that of his fellow. Once again, the exegetes are divided. Yosef Kara (whose position usually reflects that of Rashi who, curiously, offered no resolution to this dilemma) inferred from Ahijah's tearing "the new robe he was wearing" that it was his own, while Radak openly acknowledged "either Ahijah or Jeroboam, it is indeterminate."

Outstanding, in this respect, is the commentary of Yosef Ibn Kaspi, a contemporary of Ralbag and a fellow Provençal, who disambiguated the verses and provided an explanation for the tearing of the cloak.

Most correctly, [the robe] belonged to Ahijah, since it was customary for prophets to wear a cloak. Furthermore, the verse [30] calls it "the new robe he was wearing" and does not call it "Jeroboam's robe." Also, [the next verse] names him [implicitly] saying "he said to Jeroboam."

Moreover, those who were unblemished [spiritually] were unconcerned about tearing their clothing—even if it is new and expensive—and, in general, they are unaffected by incurring financial loss in the pursuit of spiritual perfection… While it would have been sufficient to do all this verbally, [action] is a more effective way to make an impression on the minds of the observers and listeners.

Whatever the case was, the symbolism—both here and in 1 Samuel—is the same: the undamaged robe represents wholeness; tearing it reflects separation and dissolution. Just as Samuel was signifying the rending of Saul's kingdom and its transfer to David, Ahijah, by distributing ten parts of the robe to Jeroboam, was giving him the lion's share of the Kingdom of Israel, while retaining only a minor portion for the Davidic dynasty.

1 Kings 12

The March of Folly: Rulers and Bad Advice —
With an Extended Commentary by Barbara Tuchman

In our comments on 2 Samuel 19, we observed that the Sages were perturbed over David's rash and baseless decision to have Mephi-Boshet split his property with Tziva, and we noted a Midrash (cited by Radak) stating that it caused a heavenly voice (*bat kol*) to announce the eventual division of David's kingdom amongst Rehoboam, his

FIRST KINGS

grandson, and Jeroboam ben Nebat. The proverbial chickens have come home to roost in our chapter.

This episode also features prominently in the preface to a most intriguing book: *The March of Folly,* by Pulitzer Prize-winning author Barbara W. Tuchman. In Chapter One, entitled "Pursuit of Policy Contrary to Self-Interest," she offers Rehoboam's rejection of a tax cut as evidence of how often leaders act foolishly—particularly when more wholesome alternatives are readily available. (The book is subtitled: *"From Troy to Vietnam."*) Let these excerpts from her description of this event (pp. 9-10) serve as our lesson:

> Acknowledged king without question by the two southern tribes of Judah and Benjamin, Rehoboam, clearly aware of unrest in Israel, traveled at once to Shechem, center of the north, to obtain the people's allegiance. He was met instead by a delegation of Israel's representatives who demanded that he lighten the heavy yoke of labor put upon them by his father and said that if he did so they would serve him as loyal subjects [4]. Among the delegates was Jeroboam who had hurriedly been sent for from Egypt as soon as King Solomon died, and whose presence must certainly have warned Rehoboam that he faced a critical situation.
>
> ... With the first sensation of sovereignty heating his blood, Rehoboam found this advice [of the older counselors—to be lenient] too tame and turned to "the young men that were grown up with him" [8]. They knew his disposition and like counselors of any time who wish to consolidate their position in the "Oval Office," gave advice they knew would be palatable...
>
> Delighted with this ferocious formula ["my father chastised you with whips, I will chastise you with scorpions" 11], Rehoboam faced the delegation when it returned on the

third day and addressed them "roughly" [13], word for word as the young men had suggested...

Instantly—so instantly as to suggest that they had previously decided upon their course of action in case of a negative reply—the men of Israel announced their secession from the House of David with the battle cry "To thy tents, O Israel! See to thine own house, David" [16].

1 Kings 13

Setting Limits on Prophecy

Two items in this chapter related to prophecy invite interpretation. In verse 2, "the man of God"—rabbinic tradition, based on 2 Chronicles 9:29, identified him as Ido the Seer—delivered the following oracle:

> O altar, altar! Thus said the Lord: A son shall be born (*nolad*) to the House of David, Josiah by name; and he shall slaughter upon you the priests of the shrines who bring offerings upon you. And human bones shall be burned upon you.

First, why did he address the altar twice? Here, we have a classic confrontation between *peshat* (literary and linguistic interpretation) and *derash* (homily). Radak explained that the repetition of the name of something in direct address is standard for Tanakh and cited, in evidence, "Abraham Abraham" (Genesis 22:11), "Jacob Jacob" (Gen. 46:2), "Moses Moses" (Exodus 3:4), and "Samuel Samuel" (1 Samuel 3:10). Rashi, however, explained that he was simply referring to two altars: that which he stood before in Bethel and the other, which stood in Dan. We can ask: which is the *peshat* and which is the *derash*?

Second, a close reading of the Hebrew text reveals a problem with our translation. The verb *nolad* designates the past tense; the future tense would require *yivvaled*. Since Josiah would not be born for several hundred years, why speak of his birth as though it had already occurred? An answer to this question comes to us from Don Isaac Abravanel (15-16th century, Spain and Italy):

> This verse teaches us important fundamentals. First, that prophets saw matters that came to them in [a divine] flow in detail, rather than the flow being [only] of generalities and the imagination of the prophet filling in the details—as is maintained by recent Jewish philosophers. If that were the case, this prophet would not have perceived who of the House of David would perform these actions, nor that his name would be Josiah, since it would not occur for many years.

In all candor, I must admit to finding this somewhat unsatisfactory. Even granting the prophetic ability to foretell the future in precise detail, I cannot imagine of what value the name of Josiah could have had to the immediate audience. Perhaps prophets had a sense that their words would be preserved for later generations?

1 Kings 14

"And Me You Have Cast Behind Your Back"

In the previous chapter, we heard the oracle pronounced by "the man of God" condemning Jeroboam and his descendants to a fiery end because he promoted worship and sacrifice at the high places (*bamot*). Here we begin to see its fulfillment. When Jeroboam's son took ill, he sent his wife to consult Ahijah, the very same prophet who had earlier chosen him to rule over the ten tribes. Although Jeroboam instructed her to travel incognito, Ahijah was forewarned by God of her approach, and he greeted her with, "Come in, wife of Jeroboam. Why are you disguised? I have a harsh message for you" (6). Implicitly, Jeroboam feared that Ahijah would respond to him severely regardless of the actual inquiry, and that fear was confirmed. Even without hearing her question about the fate of the child, he warned her that his message would be "harsh."

Ahijah then proceeded to enumerate God's charges against Jeroboam, who had been promoted to king in order to enhance the service of God. Instead, "You have acted worse than all those who preceded you; you have gone and made for yourself other gods and molten images to vex Me; and Me you have cast behind your back" (9).

Who were "all those" who preceded Jeroboam? After all, the total number of kings who had ruled over Israel by this point in time was three: Saul, David, and Solomon. Saul failed God in his inability to confront Amalek as instructed (1 Samuel 15), David sinned grievously in the matter of Bathsheba and Uriah (2 Samuel 11–12), and of Solomon we read:

> In his old age, his wives turned away Solomon's heart after other gods, and he was not as wholeheartedly devoted to the Lord his God as his father David had been. Solomon followed Ashtoreth the goddess of the Phoenicians, and Milcom the abomination of the Ammonites. Solomon did what was displeasing to the Lord and did not remain loyal to the Lord like his father David (1 Kings 11:4–6).

How could Jeroboam have "acted worse"? I suspect that the answer resides in the phrase with which we entitled these remarks: "And Me you have cast behind your back" (v. 9). Saul, David, and even Solomon's faith in God never wavered, however susceptible to error they may have been. Jeroboam was of another type; he set God aside, as it were, and pretended He was not there. For the former kings, repentance and redemption were lively possibilities; for Jeroboam, they were dead letters.

1 Kings 15

Bubbie Maacah: How to Understand the Convoluted Family Relationships of Abijam and Asa

At the close of the previous chapter, almost as an afterthought to the story of Jeroboam, we read about Rehoboam and how, under his reign, the people of Judah committed many of the same crimes that were being committed elsewhere in Israel under Jeroboam. At the very end of the chapter, Rehoboam died and was succeeded by his son Abijam. Here is where our chapter picks up the narrative thread, and here is where we get entangled in a web of seemingly incompatible identities.

According to verse 2, Abijam's mother was Maacah daughter of Abishalom. Yet, when he died and was succeeded by his son Asa, we read in verse 10 that Asa's mother was also named Maacah daughter of Abishalom. To complicate matters further, the parallel passage in 2 Chronicles reports that Abijah's mother was Micaiah the daughter of Uriel (13:2), while Asa's mother is still listed as Maacah (16).

Unless Abijah and Asa were brothers, rather than father and son—something that runs counter to the explicit sense of the biblical text and must be discounted—how can we reconcile these discrepancies? Indeed, Radak offered more than one way out of this maze. In his commentary to 2 Chronicles 13:2, he wrote:

> Micaiah bat Uriel is Maacah bat Abishalom mentioned above (11:20). Both she and her father were known by two names.

> [The names] Micaiah and Maacah resemble one another. There are many such instances in this book wherein one person is known by two names.

However, in his commentary to our chapter he wrote:

> Maacah was not Asa's mother, but his grandmother, and a grandmother can also be called a mother... [Scripture] related Asa to his grandmother because she worshipped idols... and yet he did right in the eyes of God and did not follow her.

Indeed, we read further in our chapter about Asa: "He also deposed his mother Maacah from the rank of queen mother, because she had made an abominable thing for [the goddess] Asherah. Asa cut down her abominable thing and burnt it in the Wadi Kidron" (13).

NB: In a note to our comments on chapter 3, we cited "a trope that will recur throughout the Book of Kings: A king will be acknowledged for all his meritorious deeds, but a caveat will follow to the effect that 'however, the platforms were not removed; the people continued offering sacrifices and incense on the platforms.'" Verse 14 of our chapter is but the first.

1 Kings 16

What Goes Around...
Conspiracies and Plots Plague the Kingship

We read at the close of the previous chapter that Jeroboam died and was succeeded by his son Nadav, who ruled for two years and followed in the evil footsteps of his father (15:25–26). He then became the victim of a conspiracy (*kesher*, see 15:27) that placed on the throne of the Northern Kingdom a "man of Issachar" named Baasha, who exacted from the House of Jeroboam the precise vengeance that had been foretold (in chapter 13) by the man of God and confirmed by Ahijah of Shiloh (chapter 14). Despite that, "He did what was displeasing to the Lord; he followed the ways of Jeroboam and the sins which he caused Israel to commit" (15:34).

When our chapter opens, another prophet, Jehu ben Hanani, prophesied that Baasha was about to suffer the very same fate he meted out to Nadav and Jeroboam:

| Anyone belonging to Jeroboam who dies in the town shall be devoured by dogs, and anyone who dies in the open country shall be eaten by the birds of the sky; for the Lord has spoken. (14:11) | Anyone belonging to Baasha who dies in the town shall be devoured by dogs, and anyone belonging to him who dies in the open country shall be devoured by the birds of the sky. (16:4) |

Conspiracy (*kesher*, see 16:9, 16, 20) also struck again as Baasha's son Elah was slain by Zimri, one of his officers. Zimri, after exacting the prophesied vengeance on the House of Baasha, became the victim of a conspiracy himself as the people chose a general named Omri to ascend the throne. Omri besieged the royal palace at Tirzah, and Zimri (to spite Omri?) burned it down about himself after ruling for just one week.

Omri eventually moved his capital to Samaria (Shomron), which became an epithet for the Northern Kingdom (and remains in use to this very day to designate Israeli-held territory within the northern West Bank), and established a new dynasty whose most famous (or infamous) member, Ahab, makes his appearance just as our chapter is about to close.

IN THE COMPANY OF PROPHETS

1 Kings 17

Elijah the Tishbite, an Inhabitant Of Gilead: Who Was He Really?

Few biblical characters have had as long a shelf life as Elijah the Prophet. He is said to be present annually at the Seder, weekly at the close of Shabbat, and the seat occupied by whoever holds a child during his circumcision is named for him. On the other hand, he has no back story: he bursts upon the scene in the very first verse of our chapter and launches into his condemnation of Ahab without as much as an introduction, save for the spare remarks we have used as the title for these comments: "Elijah the Tishbite, an inhabitant of Gilead." How much more can we presume to know?

First of all, a closer look at the original text is in order, lest we lose sight of the fact that Elijah was both a *toshav* (Hebrew for "inhabitant") of the Gilead region and a *tishbi*—arguably, a resident of a placed called *Toshav*, perhaps situated within the Gilead.

Next, we look at the Gilead itself, which we know from both the Torah (Numbers 32) and the Book of Joshua (22) to have been settled by the tribes of Reuben, Gad, and half of Manasseh, making it likely—though far from certain—that Elijah belonged to one of those tribes.

With these data in hand, let us now see how Radak performed the identification.

> Our Sages were divided over his tribal affiliation. Some said he was of the tribe of Gad, while others said he was of Benjamin, and yet others said that Phinehas [the Priest] was Elijah. Each of them relied on [the evidence] of verses, however far-fetched. We, however, do not know with certainty.

The affiliation with Gad is clearly the most reasonable of the three possibilities and is supported by the biblical evidence we cited just above. The association with Benjamin (appearing in the *Midrash Sekhel Tov*) is based on the appearance of the name Eliyah in 1 Chronicles 8, amongst Benjamin's descendants. The identification with Phinehas is based on the quality of zealousness they shared. Elijah: "I have been truly zealous for the Lord" (1 Kings 19:10) and Phinehas: "Because he was zealous for his God" (Numbers 25:13).

It is likely that it was with this final association in mind that Malachi, the last of the prophets, declared: "Behold I will send to you Elijah the Prophet, prior to the coming of the great and awesome day of the Lord" (3:23).

1 Kings 18

Elijah the Reviver:
But What Does CPR Have to Do with Making It Rain?

At the close of the previous chapter, Elijah performed an (apparent) miracle: He resuscitated the (ostensibly) dead child of the widow with whom he was residing.

The parentheses reflect an opinion among the medieval commentaries that the child had not actually died. To recall our comments on the previous chapter, there were those who believed Elijah was one and the same as Phinehas and, as a priest, he would have been forbidden to touch a corpse. Thus, the child had not actually died but—perhaps—had suffered only respiratory arrest. Of course, an obvious alternative explanation—utilizing the selfsame facts—is to argue that the mitzvah of rescue (*pikuach nefesh*) overrode that prohibition.

IN THE COMPANY OF PROPHETS

Our chapter opens in the third year of the drought that Elijah had invoked, with God instructing him to "Go, appear before Ahab; then I will send rain upon the earth" (1). Do you see a connection to the conclusion of the previous chapter? Malbim saw them as two related examples of revival:

> The opinion of the Sages is well-known: When [Elijah] required the keys of resurrection, he [first] needed to return the keys to the rain.... At first, Elijah sealed all the conduits of abundance [*tzinorot ha-shefa'*, likely a Kabbalistic term for the linkage between heaven and earth] that provided rain and sustenance, so he no longer had the ability to restore life to anything because that necessitated the opening of a conduit. However, while attempting to revive the child, he needed to renege on his sealing of the flow and that reopened all the life-giving sources that had been sealed off together with the rain.

In the interim, and unbeknownst to Elijah, Ahab had been scouring the earth for him. (Such, at least, is the literal meaning of v. 10.) Ahab had employed the services of the righteous Obadiah to secure a royal appearance by Elijah and to beseech the prophet to end the drought. In this regard, we encounter a most curious exchange. Elijah said to Obadiah, "Go tell your master, Elijah is here" (8), to which Obadiah responded, "When I leave you, the spirit of the Lord will carry you off I don't know where; and when I come and tell Ahab and he does not find you, he will kill me" (12). Granted that Elijah might have preferred to avoid Ahab's company, but once he had made an appointment to see him, why might he fail to keep it?

As a member of Hatzalah, a volunteer rescue service, for more than thirty years, I think I have an insight into Elijah's seemingly rude behavior. He, too, was a first responder (he arguably performed the first recorded act of CPR), and even if he were on his way to meet the king, if his emergency beeper went off—he was duty-bound to go wherever it took him.

1 Kings 19

Now, Lord, Take My Life!
Did Elijah Have Suicidal Ideation?

Our chapter reports on the consequences to Elijah of his stunning triumph over the priests of Baal that was described in the previous chapter. Jezebel put a price on his head, and he was forced to flee to the wilderness, implying that even a retreat to the Kingdom of Judah was not sufficiently secure. To wit: "He himself went a day's journey into the wilderness. He came to a broom bush [or juniper tree] and sat down under it and prayed that he might die. 'Enough!' he cried. 'Now, O Lord, take my life, for I am no better than my fathers'" (4).

Why would a prophet of God—moreover, a man who had demonstrably triumphed over death (see chapter 17)—now seek it for himself? Some of the classic exegetes explained this unusual behavior as follows.

Radak suggested that Elijah was not necessarily intent on dying; rather, he was offering God the choice of either taking his life or extricating him from his predicament. He had already lived longer than any of his ancestors, and that supports the supposition that he was Phinehas (see our comments on Chapter 17).

Ralbag observed that his seeking death implied that he, too, was suffering from the famine for which his own declaration of drought was responsible. Ralbag also adduced this verse as evidence that Elijah was Phinehas, and not only did God not accede to his request to die at that moment, but he is still alive!

Malbim began by astutely observing that the verb "he came" (*va-yavo*) means arrival at a destination, which implies that Elijah was not wandering randomly about the wilderness but was headed for a specific location only "one day's journey" away. Malbim also noted that Elijah's request was not self-destructive but was intended (rhetorically?) to ascertain whether he had fulfilled his life's mission.

In light of the fact that there is no subsequent record of Elijah's death, only of his ascent (alive?) to heaven in a fiery chariot (2 Kings 2), coupled with his ubiquity at key ritual occasions (see our opening comments to 1 Kings 17), the rabbinic and medieval speculation over his lifespan is all the more poignant.

1 Kings 20

Hit Me — Or Else?
An Object Lesson in the Consequences of Disobedience

This chapter, which tells of the miraculous victory that God granted Ahab over the forces of Aram, contains, inter alia, one exceptionally memorable phrase and one particularly perplexing incident.

The memorable phrase is part of Ahab's retort to Ben-Hadad, King of Aram, "Let not him who girds on [his sword] boast like him who ungirds it!" (11). It has become an oft-quoted maxim cautioning against boasting about your intentions until you have accomplished something. It is rooted in military experience: one who girds on his sword has not yet tasted battle, while he who ungirds it is a combat veteran.

The perplexing incident involves the anonymous prophet-in-training (we will deal with his identity below) who asked to be beaten (35ff.). We eventually learn that he wanted to appear before the king disheveled and bruised as though he had been engaged in combat, but how could he have pronounced a death sentence on a fellow (36) simply for his failure to play along with his charade?

Rashi, Radak, and Malbim were all essentially in agreement here. They suggested that since the prophet's message to Ahab was that he deserved to be punished for his failure to obey his instructions to kill Ben-Hadad, he made the fellow who refused to strike him an object lesson for the consequences of disobedience. They assumed that his prophetic status was recognized by the other, so his refusal to comply was not just a personal affront—which might well have gone unanswered—but an offense against God, the prophet's principal. Indeed, his request, as reported by Scripture, included "at the word of the Lord" (35).

As to the identity of the prophet who assured Ahab his victory (13), a rabbinic tradition (*Seder Olam Rabbah* 20) identified him with Micayhu ben Yimla, who makes a cameo appearance in Chapter 22. There, his advice was sought by the righteous king of Judah, Jehoshaphat, while wicked Ahab refused even to see him, complaining, ironically, that "I hate him, because he never prophesies anything good for me, but only misfortune" (22:8).

1 Kings 21

What Did Naboth Do Wrong and What Did Ahab Do Right?

Exploring the Suffering of the Righteous, and the Prospering of the Not at All Righteous

In our chapter, wicked King Ahab and wicked Queen Jezebel conspired to acquire a desirable piece of private property (a vineyard) by eliminating its owner (Naboth) and then exercising their royal prerogative to make it their own. This unholy transaction provided the prophet Elijah with the opportunity to utter a singular accusation: "Would you murder and take possession?" (19), an expression that has been utilized throughout the ages to designate a particularly nefarious deed that has illicitly enriched its perpetrator.

A question not often asked of this episode involves the victim, Naboth the Jezreelite. Based on the assumption that God is always just, Naboth's death begs justification beyond the obvious wickedness of Ahab and Jezebel. What did he do to deserve to be the victim of this conspiracy? A classical Midrash provides an answer:

> "Honor the Lord from your treasure" (*hon'kha*) (Proverbs 3:9) is to be read as "from your gifts" (*chen'kha*). If you have a pleasant voice and you are present in a synagogue, honor the Lord with your voice. Naboth [the Jezreelite] had a pleasant voice. At pilgrimage times, all Israel would gather in Jerusalem to hear his voice. Once upon a time, he did not make the pilgrimage and the corrupt witnesses testified against him and he was lost. What caused this? His failure to make the pilgrimage to Jerusalem to honor God with what He had gifted him (*Pesikta Rabbati* 25).

The continuation of the story also begs interpretation. "When Ahab heard these words [Elijah's prophecy of doom], he rent his clothes and put sackcloth on his body. He fasted and lay in sackcloth and walked about subdued" (27), whereupon God declared "Because he has humbled himself before Me, I will not bring the disaster in his lifetime; I will bring the disaster upon his house in his son's time" (29). Naboth, an ostensibly righteous man, missed a single pilgrimage and suffered death, while Ahab, of whom our chapter says, "There never was anyone like Ahab, who committed himself to doing what was displeasing to the Lord" (25) experienced momentary regret and had his sentence suspended.

No wonder the question of theodicy—commonly phrased as "the righteous suffer while the wicked prosper"—remains a perennial challenge to believers.

1 Kings 22

Another Prophetic Face Off: Micaiah Is the One Telling the Truth — Most of the Time...

Back in Chapter 18, we witnessed Elijah win a contest that pitted him against 450 prophets of Baʿal and 400 prophets of Asherah. Now, we are witness to yet another face-off, this time pitting another single true prophet, Micaiah ben Imla, against 400 other prophets, perhaps the same 400 prophets of Asherah who escaped their fate previously. The subject? Should the combined forces of the two kingdoms of Israel launch a coordinated attack against Aram.

The messenger who was dispatched to summon Micaiah attempted to put his finger on the scale, so to speak, by intimating that Micaiah should join in the chorus of the other prophets and support the attack. Micaiah, however, replied, "I will speak only what the Lord tells me" (14).

When he came before the king, the king said to him, "Micaiah, shall we march upon Ramoth-Gilead for battle, or shall we not?" He answered him, "March and triumph! The Lord will deliver [it] into Your Majesty's hands." The king said to him, "How many times must I adjure you to tell me nothing but the truth in the name of the Lord?" Then he said, "I saw all Israel scattered over the hills like sheep without a shepherd; and the Lord said, 'These have no master; let everyone return to his home in safety.'" "Didn't I tell you," said the king of Israel to Jehoshaphat, "that he would not prophesy good fortune for me, but only misfortune?" (15–18)

Arguably, the only king who spoke here was Ahab, who is clearly the subject of the final verse, in which he addressed Jehoshaphat. This would imply that Ahab was also the only king to be addressed here by Micaiah (see our comments to Chapter 20). However, this raises the question of how the prophet could have initially endorsed the plan, only to renege on his endorsement, if, indeed, he was constrained to speak only what the Lord told him.

The answer, which is predicated upon a really close reading of verses 15 and 17, was supplied by Rashi, who pointed out that in verse 15 Micaiah did not speak in God's name, while in verse 17 he explicitly stated, "the Lord said."

Second Kings

Giuseppe Angeli, *Elijah Taken Up in a Chariot of Fire* (c. 1740)

2 Kings 1

A Hairy Man with a Leather Belt Tied Around His Waist

Why Did the Emissaries Not Recognize This Distinctive Figure?

In yet another of a number of encounters between prophets and people who seek prognoses of their illnesses (see, inter alia, 1 Kings 17 and 2 Kings 8), Elijah intercepted the emissaries of King Ahaziah and diverted them from their intended destination: Baal-Zebub, the deity of the Philistine city of Ekron, literally "Lord of the Flies" (as in the William Golding novel) but—in Aramaic—a common noun meaning enemy. In response to the king's subsequent interrogation, they identified their interlocutor as "a hairy man… with a leather belt tied around his waist," whom Ahaziah immediately identified as "Elijah the Tishbite" (8).

Was the giveaway the hair or the belt, and was Elijah the only man in Israel who matched that description? And if he, indeed, was so distinctive as to be immediately recognizable, why did the emissaries not recognize him? In answering these questions, Radak managed to connect several of the dots that have led us here since we were first introduced to Elijah in 1 Kings 17. He wrote:

> [The king] recognized [Elijah's] habit of wearing a leather belt and [also] knew that he was hairy. It is curious that the emissaries of the king of Israel did not recognize him when he was accustomed to spending time with Ahab in Samaria. It is possible that these men whom the king of Israel dispatched were not present in Samaria at the time that Elijah was

regularly there. It was also quite some time since he had been there because Jezebel had ordered his death (1 Kings 19:2). Indeed, during the war against Ben-Hadad (1 Kings 20) we did not see him there, nor during the war of Ramot Gilead when Micaiah ben Yimla served as God's prophet in Samaria (1 Kings 22).

A particularly poignant note was struck here by Yosef Ibn Kaspi (Provence; 14th century), who identified the leather belt as one that was worn above all of one's other clothes. He had visited the Holy Land and interpolated some of its realia into his commentaries. He wrote: "It is the custom of that land to this very day to wear a belt over all their clothes," which, possibly, were robes rather than separate shirts and pants.

2 Kings 2

"Oh, Father, Father! Israel's Chariots and Horsemen!" Memorable Eulogy — But What Does This Mean?

When Elijah first encountered Elisha, he was plowing with twelve yokes of oxen (1 Kings 19:19). When he threw his mantle over him, Elisha left his oxen and ran after him, saying "Let me kiss my father and mother good-by, and I will follow you," suggesting, perhaps, that Elisha saw Elijah as a surrogate parent. Small wonder, then, that when Elijah and Elisha parted company permanently, the latter referred to the former as his "father." Less obvious is the meaning of "Israel's chariots and horsemen" (12). Let us sample what the medieval commentaries had to say on the description of this relationship.

Rashi, in appreciation of the fact that the relationship between masters and disciples is akin to that of fathers and sons, wrote: "My endeared teacher who is better for Israel with his prayers than chariots and horsemen." Radak echoed Rashi, adding that on account of this relationship prophets in training were called "sons of prophets" (see vs. 3, 5, and 15 in this chapter).

Gersonides (Ralbag) added the explanation that a teacher "fathers" a student's intellect (*sekhel*) and adduced the balance of the verse—"he grasped his garments and rent them in two"—as evidence that a disciple is obliged to tear his garments on the death of his teacher. In fact, according to Ralbag, whereas an ordinary mourner may, eventually, reattach the pieces of his torn garment, the disciple may never do so.

Concerning the chariot (*rekheb*), Malbim saw an allusion to an esoteric notion—called "Merkabah mysticism" by scholars—that alludes to God's providence (*hashgahah*) over Israel and identified Elijah as an agent of that providence.

2 Kings 3

"Now King Mesha of Moab Was a Sheep Breeder" And We Have the Archaeological Proof

In this chapter, we encounter the historical figure Mesha, King of Moab. Not that Ben-Hadad of Aram (see 1 Kings 20) was unhistorical, but Mesha is unique in respect of the fact that we have extra-biblical evidence of his existence in the form of a monumental inscription called The Mesha Stele. Comprising 30 lines of text inscribed on a black basalt stone, it describes Mesha's victories over Israel—particularly those that occurred after the death of King Ahab of Israel—just as recounted here.

An endearing feature of the stele is its accessibility. Written in the Moabite language and in the same script that served Hebrew in the biblical period, it can be read by anyone who has a reasonable acquaintance with biblical Hebrew. Here, for example (and in transliteration), are its opening words: *anokhi mesha' ben kemosh melek moab hadiboni*, or "I am Mesha (v.4), son of Kemosh (the national god of Moab; Numbers 21:29, Judges 11:24), king of Moab, the Dibonite (the capital of Moab; Numbers 21:30, Joshua 13:9)." In the continuation, Mesha referred directly to the king of Israel, writing: *umelekh yisrael banah et yahatz, vayeshev bah behiltahamoh bi, vayegarshehu kemosh mipanai* (lines 18–19): "The king of Israel built Yahatz (Numbers 21:23, Deut. 2:32) and dwelt there while he fought against me, [however] Kemosh chased him out before me."

The inscription was discovered in Diban, Jordan, in 1868, by Bedouin who broke it into pieces to prevent it falling into the hands of the infidel Christians. Nevertheless, it was deciphered by the French Consul, Clermont Ganeau, an avid archaeologist, who was able to put it back together. It was later transferred to the Louvre in Paris where it remains.

[Breaking news: After these remarks were originally published on "929," Israeli scholars reversed an earlier reading of l.31 of the stele, changing a tentative identification of *bt [d]vd* (the House of David) to *blq*, referencing Balak, King of Moab, who hired the Midianite sorcerer Balaam to curse Israel (Numbers 22–24).]

2 Kings 4

Elijah Reprised and Surpassed
Elisha Has Clearly Mastered the Tricks of the Trade

When Elijah was about to part company from Elisha, he granted his disciple a wish: "Tell me, what can I do for you before I am taken from you?" Elisha replied: "Let a double portion of your spirit pass on to me" (2 Kings 2:9). If we are not inclined to view this as an act of hubris, it most likely signified that Elisha regarded himself as being only half the man of God that Elijah was; therefore, he would need twice his master's spirit in order to accomplish just as much. In our chapter, we find Elisha reprising some of Elijah's activities.

In the chapter in which we were first introduced to Elijah, he performed a miracle to provide food for a woman of Tzarfat. In the words of his prophetic message, "The jar of flour shall not give out and the jug of oil shall not fail until the day that the Lord sends rain upon the ground" (1 Kings 17:14). In our chapter (3ff.), we find Elisha miraculously providing sustenance for the widow of a prophet-in-training.

Even more striking, perhaps, was Elisha's duplication of his master's successful resuscitation of an apparently dead child. Elijah brought back to life the son of the woman of Tzarfat after "he had no breath left in him" (1 Kings 17:17), and, in our chapter, Elisha breathed life back into the son of the Shunamite woman with whom he was boarding ,"and the boy opened his eyes" (35). It is significant that in each of the two cases cited here the prophet first uttered a prayer to God before actually performing artificial respiration. Indeed, the failure of Gehazi, Elisha's manservant, to succeed in his attempt to revive the child would argue that more was involved here than just the exercise of CPR.

In addition, towards the end of the chapter, Elisha rescued a stew from poisonous gourds by mixing in flour (reminiscent of Moses saving the water at Marah by tossing in a branch, cf. Exodus 15:25). He then replicated his earlier miracle by enabling a small amount of food to feed one hundred people, "and when they had eaten, they [even] had some left over" (v. 43), arguably a manifestation of "a double portion" of Elijah's spirit.

IN THE COMPANY OF PROPHETS

2 Kings 5

Elisha and Some Prophetic Shenanigans:
What Do We Look for in a Prophet: Oratory or Activism?

In this chapter, Elisha performed a major miracle and a series of minor wonders that make us contemplate what prophecy is all about.

Elisha startled Naaman by suggesting that Naaman cure his leprosy* by bathing in the Jordan. Naaman was offended because he saw the Jordan as inferior to the rivers of his homeland, Aram. (This is reminiscent of Mark Twain, who thought the Jordan would eclipse the Mississippi and was flabbergasted to discover that he could stand on one side of it and spit across to the other.) However, after acceding to the prophet's instruction, "his flesh became like a little boy's, and he was clean" (14). Removing leprosy (or, for that matter, initiating it) is something the Torah associates with Moses (see Exodus 4:6–7) and can rightfully be regarded as major league prophetic ability.

The force of this miracle, however, seems to be blunted by a succession of relatively minor deeds—related to us over the course of this chapter and the next—that cast Elisha more as a wizard than a man of God. First, he saw through Gehazi's attempt to cover up his unauthorized shakedown of Naaman (5:25ff.); then, he enabled a prophetic trainee to reattach a lost axe head to its shaft (6:6–7); next, he blinded the Assyrian posse pursuing him and led them straight into captivity in Samaria (6:18ff.); and, finally, he contrived to learn of a royal plot to assassinate him in time to have it frustrated by trapping its executioner in a doorway (6:32).

Where are the passionate words of rebuke and consolation we have come to expect from prophets? Indeed, what manner of prophet was

SECOND KINGS

Elisha—or, for that matter, his master, Elijah? This is an opportunity to draw a distinction between such prophets as Samuel, Nathan, Gad, Elijah, and Elisha, who were dispatched to undertake particular missions—commonly social or political in nature, on account of which they are sometimes called "apostolic" prophets—and those, like Isaiah, Jeremiah, or Ezekiel, whose assignments were more culturally or religiously based and therefore required more oratory than activism.

* Leprosy, a skin affliction known as Hansen's disease, is not identical with the biblical *tzara'at*, which was incurred on account of sin, was not contagious, and required a *kohen*, rather than a physician, to remove.

2 Kings 6

A Closer Look at a "Miracle"

In the previous chapter, we referred to the incident in which Elisha recovered the axe head that had fallen off its handle when one of the prophet-trainees was chopping wood near the Jordan River. As the text describes the salvage operation: "Where did it fall?" asked the man of God. He showed him the spot; and he cut off a stick and threw it in, and he made the ax head float" (6:6). But why did Elisha need to fashion a brand new "stick" when he could have used the one from which the metal head had been dislodged? The consensus of commentators, medieval and modern alike, is that this magnified the miraculous nature of the process. Here are some of their insights.

Radak wrote:

> Why did he need to carve a new stick? It appears that miracles require new materials—as in the [previous] case of the new cruse (2 Kings 2:20). So, he carved a stick to serve as a handle

for the axe head that had fallen off, and it fit into the socket of the axe head and they floated [to the surface] together.

In other words, if he had used the existing handle, someone might have suspected trickery. Using a handle that had never been in contact with the axe head reinforced the miraculous nature of the event.

Ralbag (Gersonides) and Malbim, however, shift the emphasis from the newness of the stick to the way the entire salvage operation transpired in defiance of nature. To cite Malbim (whose commentary here is considerably more succinct):

> This demonstrates that the prophet can reverse nature: the stick and the axe head switched their natural properties. The wood sank in the deep water like lead, while the axe head floated to the top as though it were light wood.

2 Kings 7

Lepers at the Gate
Some Clear Hints to Their Surprising Identity

There is a mathematical theorem that postulates that "things equal to the same thing are equal to each other." In alphabetical terms, if A=B and B=C, then A=C. According to rabbinic and medieval exegesis, there is an instance of this equivalence in this chapter.

The discovery that the Aramean army had miraculously fled in the middle of the night was made by "four men, lepers, outside the gate" of Samaria (3). Rashi, relaying a talmudic tradition (*Sotah* 47a), identified them as "Gehazi and his sons." Since Gehazi and his sons were lepers, and the men who made the salvific discovery were lepers, the axiom would have us identify them with one another.

We recall that Gehazi had disobeyed Elisha and, by ruse, had extracted a gift from Naaman for the curing of his leprosy (2 Kings 5:20ff.), earning the prophet's curse: "Surely, the leprosy of Naaman shall cling to you and to your descendants forever" (there, v. 27). They were situated outside the city gate in accordance with the Torah law that confines a leper to "the outskirts of the camp" (Leviticus 13:46) and consistent with the Mishnaic stipulation that "walled cities are of a higher sanctity; therefore, lepers are evicted from them" (*Kelim* 1:7).

A close reading of our chapter indicates that these four harbingers of salvation decided, on the one hand, to share the news with their brethren in the city lest they incur "guilt" (9, arguably by prolonging the famine), and yet, on the other hand, still took the time not only to slake their own thirst and hunger but to carry off silver and gold and clothing from the abandoned Assyrian camp and bury it for later retrieval (8). Who would be better suited for this role than Gehazi, whose take from Naaman consisted of silver and clothing?

It is ironic, of course, that Elisha, who had the well-deserved reputation of curing lepers (5:3), inflicted it on his own assistant. In any case, it appears that Gehazi's role in hastening the end to the siege was redemptive, since in the very next chapter we find him in direct conversation with no less than the king himself (8:4), something that clearly implies a resolution of his leprosy.

2 Kings 8

Was the King Assassinated? Or Was It a Negligent Suicide? In Trying to Resolve the Ambiguity, Textual and Contextual Clues Point in Different Directions

A sizable portion of this chapter is devoted to the incident in which Elisha revealed to Hazael, an Aramean officer, that his king, Ben-Hadad, would die of his current illness and that he, Hazael, would succeed him. He cautioned Hazael, however, to engage in a subterfuge and to tell Ben-Hadad that he would recuperate. (Although he prophesied that Hazael will do "harm" to the Israelite people, one gets the sense that the prophet's candor was intended to offset that as much as possible.)

When Hazael returned home and the king asked him, "What did Elisha say to you?" he replied, "He told me, 'You shall surely live'" (14). Then Scripture narrates, "The next day, he took a piece of netting, dipped it in water, and spread it over his face. So [Ben-Hadad] died, and Hazael succeeded him as king" (15). There is an ambiguity here: Who spread the wet netting over Ben-Hadad's face?

Methodologically speaking, there are two principal ways to resolve ambiguities, which I shall call the textual and the contextual. The textual approach adheres closely to the accepted rules of grammar and syntax, which, in this case, dictate that the subject of "he took a piece of netting" is one and the same with the previous verb "he told me," namely Hazael; so it was Hazael who smothered the king by placing the wet netting on his face.

Contextually, however, since Hazael trusted Elisha's forecast, why would he put himself at risk by precipitating Ben-Hadad's death? Thus, the more reasonable explanation is that Ben-Hadad, believing that he would recover, imprudently placed a wet cloth on his own face and died as a result, thereby confirming Elisha's prognosis and leaving the way clear for Hazael to assume the throne without raising any doubts about his loyalty and without endangering his succession.

SECOND KINGS

2 Kings 9

"Is All Well, Zimri, Murderer of Your Master?"
Ahab and Jezebel Get Their Just Desserts

"What goes around—come around." That is the contemporary equivalent of the rabbinic expression, "By the measure with which one metes out, so is it meted out to him" (Mishnah *Sotah* 1:7), and what literary types may call poetic justice. In this chapter, we witness a reversal of the fortunes of the House of Ahab.

Elijah had cautioned his royal nemesis that "I will bring disaster upon you. I will make a clean sweep of you, I will cut off from Israel every male belonging to Ahab, bond and free" (1 Kings 21:21). In this chapter, Elisha's appointed messenger, in anointing Jehu to succeed Jehoram son of Ahab, announced: "The whole House of Ahab shall perish, and I will cut off every male belonging to Ahab, bond and free in Israel" (8). In that earlier warning, Elijah had said: "In the very place where the dogs lapped up Naboth's blood [i.e., his field in Jezreel], the dogs will lap up your blood too" (1 Kings 21:19), and in this chapter the messenger said: "The dogs shall devour Jezebel in the field of Jezreel, with none to bury her" (10).

Finally, as Jehu approached, Jezebel—who, curiously, had prepared for her denouement by painting her eyes and dressing her hair (30)—sought to have the last word, addressing him (as in the title of these remarks) as Zimri, an officer who had rebelled against the earlier King Baasha, slaying him and his household (1 Kings 16:10). If Jezebel was up on her royal history—or on her Tanakh, for that matter—there might have been a twinge of sarcasm in this metaphor, given that Zimri ruled for only seven days (16:16). More intriguing, however, is the coincidence (?) that Baasha's downfall was forecast by a prophet named Jehu (16:1). Go figure.

2 Kings 10

Who Were the Rechabites?
Clan? Sect? Nazirites? Homeless?
Nomads? Separatists? Allies?

In our chapter, Jehu made common cause with Jehonadab ben Rechab: "He greeted him and said to him, 'Are you as wholehearted with me as I am with you'? 'I am', Jehonadab replied. 'If so, [said Jehu,] give me your hand.' He gave him his hand and [Jehu] helped him into the chariot" (15). Subsequently, Jehonadab participated in Jehu's stratagem to eliminate all the priests of Baal in one fell swoop (23ff.), and that is all we hear of him at this juncture.

However, the name Jehonadab ben Rechab recurs in the Book of Jeremiah. God instructed Jeremiah: "Go to the house of the Rechabites and speak to them" (35:2) and ordered him to tempt them to drink wine. The Rechabites refused, explaining:

We will not drink wine, for our ancestor, Jonadab son of Rechab, commanded us: "You shall never drink wine, either you or your children (6). Nor shall you build houses or sow fields or plant vineyards, nor shall you own such things; but you shall live in tents all your days, so that you may live long upon the land where you sojourn" (7). And we have obeyed our ancestor Jonadab son of Rechab in all that he commanded us... (8)

Both the names Jehonadab/Jonadab and Rechab also occurred previously in Tanakh. The former was the name of a wise friend of Amnon, son of King David, who advised him on how to have his way with Tamar (cf. 2 Samuel 13:3ff.), and the latter was one of a pair of officers of King Saul who betrayed Ish-Boshet, Saul's son, and delivered his head to David (2 Samuel 4:2ff.). Since the combination is unique to this chapter and to Jeremiah, the medieval exegetes were inclined to regard them as one and the same. Relying on 1 Chronicles 2:55, they also considered them to be descended from Jethro, father-in-law of Moses.

Aaron Demsky, Professor at Bar-Ilan University, captured this identification as follows:

> RECHABITES: A clan headed by Jehonadab, son of Rechab (c. 841 BCE), claiming descent from Jethro and the Kenites. The Rechabites resided among the Israelites, leading a pastoral existence, and abstaining from intoxicating drink. Zealous anti-Baalists, they cooperated with Jehu in extirpating the household of Ahab (2 Kgs. 10.15–27). They still existed in the time of Jeremiah, who held them up to the recalcitrant Judeans as an example of fidelity and self-discipline. (*The Oxford Dictionary of the Jewish Religion*, 1997, 575.)

2 Kings 11

Baal Suffers a Double Blow: The Treasonous Overthrow of the Baal-Worshiping Queen

At about the same time that Jehu was eliminating Baal worship from the northern kingdom of Samaria, events were unfolding in the southern kingdom of Judah that were leading to the identical result.

After the death of Ahaziah, King of Judah, at the hands of Jehu (2 Kings 9:27), Queen Mother Athaliah seized the opportunity to consolidate her own hold on the kingdom by killing off all the members of the royal family (1). Unbeknownst to her, Joash, the infant son of Ahaziah, was rescued and spent six years hidden away in the

Temple under the auspices of Jehoiadah, the High Priest (2–3), who eventually conspired with the loyal officers of Ahaziah to restore Joash to the throne (4ff.). Athaliah herself was executed, but not before she was able to cry out "treason, treason" (14), whose Hebrew phrasing (*kesher kesher*) links her with Jezebel's castigation of Jehu as a "Zimri" whose rebellion against Ba`asha is formally recorded as "the treason that he perpetrated" (*kishro asher kashar*; 1 Kings 16:20; see our comments there).

Jehoaidah renewed the covenant between God, the king, and the nation (17), and the people responded by shattering the altars of Baal, smashing its statues, and slaying Matan the (high?) priest of Baal. This cleared the way for the restoration of Joash to the throne (19), and "All the people of the land rejoiced, and the city was quiet" (20). Joash would continue to serve God under the tutelage of Jehoiadah (12:3), with the usual caveat (see our note to 1 Kings 3) of "The shrines [*bamot*], however, were not removed; the people continued to sacrifice and offer at the shrines" (12:4).

2 Kings 12

The First "Pushke" — Jewish Legal Precedent in the Oversight of the Collection and Distribution of Charitable Contributions

As we noted apropos of the previous chapter, Joash was a righteous king whose actions were guided by his tutelage at the hands of Jehoiada the High Priest. The one caveat to this description is that he—like nearly all the kings of Judah—tolerated the continued worship on the high platforms (*bamot*, or shrines, see 3–4). One way in which his righteousness made itself manifest was in his concern for repairing the physical plant of the Temple. Our narrative (7ff.) picks up in the

23rd year of his 40-year reign, as king and high priest confronted the reality that the priests had not obeyed their instructions and had not commissioned the necessary repairs, even though it seems that they had been collecting money for it all along.

Their solution to the problem sets a precedent that continues to be followed by Jewish organizations and in Jewish homes to this every day.

> And the priest Jehoiada took a chest and bored a hole in its lid. He placed it at the right side of the altar as one entered the House of the Lord, and the priestly guards of the threshold deposited there all the money that was brought into the House of the Lord. Whenever they saw that there was much money in the chest, the royal scribe and the high priest would come up and put the money accumulated in the House of the Lord into bags, and they would count it. Then they would deliver the money that was weighed out to the overseers of the work, who were in charge of the House of the Lord … (2 Kings 12:10–12).

Hence, we have the *pushke* (from the Polish *puszka*, meaning a "tin can"), a receptacle in which money (usually coins) intended for charitable purposes is collected and stored until it is full or there is enough to meet a particular need. Another precedent, albeit one that has not necessarily withstood the test of time, was that "No check was kept on the men to whom the money was delivered to pay the workers; for they dealt honestly" (17). *Halakhah* requires that charitable funds must be counted by two people and decisions about their distribution are to be made by three (*Bava Batra* 8b).

2 Kings 13

"I Shot an Arrow through the Air..."
Joash Fails to Understand Elisha's Subtle Message

Elisha became fatally ill and Joash, King of Israel, came to pay his respects, bemoaning Elisha's imminent departure with the identical terms used by that prophet to take leave from his own master, Elijah (2 Kings 2:12). Poignantly, Joash, who is described as not having strayed from the crimes of Jeroboam (11), paid homage to his kingdom's prophetic nemesis, while his Judean counterpart—who was also named Joash/Jehoash—did not.

Elisha used this opportunity to perform one last mission (see our description of "apostolic" prophecy in 2 Kings 5), combining it, in his customary fashion, with a miracle. He instructed the king to seize a bow and arrows and then placed his own hands over those of the king (15–16). Next, he commanded him to shoot an arrow through an eastern-facing window and declared: "An arrow of victory for the Lord! An arrow of victory over Aram!" (17).

Then, a most curious episode ensued. Elisha instructed the king to strike the ground with his remaining arrows (18), but when the latter struck but three times, the prophet got angry and accused the king of having thrown away the opportunity for total victory over Aram and settling for what can only be called a pyrrhic victory (19). Our question, of course, is: If Elisha wanted Joash to succeed, why did he not tell him how many times to strike? And since he did not tell him, how could he be angered by the fact that he struck only three times rather than five or six?

I believe that the answer lies in the declaration of victory in v. 17 (cited above), which prefaces God's victory over that of the king, and which Joash seemingly ignored. One may infer from their sequence that Elisha was intent on providing the king an opportunity to repent by soliciting his acknowledgment that it would indeed be the Lord who provided the victory, rather than the strength of arms. Also implicit in the shooting exercise was the relationship between the flight of an arrow and victory. Joash, arguably, ought to have drawn the unspoken conclusion on his own. His failure to do so indicated his unworthiness to enjoy God's support.

2 Kings 14

Conspiracy Theories: Hoist on One's Own *Kesher* — Shifting Political Alliances, Fickleness, and Violent Regime Change

Our chapter relates that once Amaziah felt secure in his reign, he set out to settle the score with "the courtiers who had assassinated his father" [Jehoash]. (5). At the close of an earlier chapter, we read that Jehoash's servants had conspired against him and murdered him (12:21). That verse featured the term *kesher* (literally, a knot; figuratively, a conspiracy), a term we have encountered on previous occasions and whose recurrence invites examination.

Our first encounter with it was in 2 Samuel 15:12, where it was used in the description of the plot that King David faced to replace him with Absalom. We next found it describing Zimri's scheme to unseat Baasha (1 Kings 16:20), and most recently in Queen Mother Athaliah's reference to her removal prior to the restoration of Jehoash to his throne (2 Kings 11:14). In other words, Jehoash, who instigated one conspiracy, became a victim of another.

Moreover, what went around, came around, and, in our chapter, Amaziah, too, became the victim of a *kesher* (19) that saw him assassinated and his son, Azariah, elevated to his throne. In the next chapter, Hoshea ben Elah will conspire against Pekah ben Remaliah and successfully displace him (15:30), only to be jailed, later, on account of another *kesher*—against his Assyrian liege lord (17:4).

The recurrence of the *kesher* phenomenon and its attestation with respect of kings of both Judah and Israel implies that the concept of monarchy was not considered sacrosanct and that political allegiances were not regarded as inviolable. Unfortunately, this fickleness extended to the people's allegiance to God, too, and we will find the major prophets inveighing against *kesher*: Isaiah (8:12); Jeremiah (11:9); and Ezekiel (22:25).

2 Kings 15

The House of Freedom or Detention? The Status of the Leper King

King Azariah (a.k.a. Uzziah) ascended the throne at the age of 16 and is credited with a reign of 52 years, even though at some point he was stricken with leprosy.* Since that must have severely limited his ability to function as king, and some of those 52 years were explicitly shared by his successors, the chronological task of determining the duration of the First Temple gets complicated. (See our remarks apropos of 1 Kings 6:1.)

At this point, I would like to tackle a singular lexicographical issue. Verse 5 stipulates that upon becoming a leper, the king took up residence in a *beit ha-chophsheet*. The Hebrew verbal root Ch-P-Sh connotes the idea of release or freedom, but what is a "House of Freedom"?

One line of investigation takes it as a euphemism. In other words, it was really a House of Detention to which he was confined, consistent with the Torah's provision for a leper: "Being unclean, he shall dwell apart; his dwelling shall be outside the camp" (Lev. 13:46).

Another line of inquiry utilizes information drawn from the language of the Canaanite port city of Ugarit, extensive portions of whose Semitic language were deciphered by scholars after its discovery in 1928. In Ugaritic (as the language is known), *beit ha-hophsheet* is a synonym for *she'ol*, the netherworld or the grave, the only place where a leper might find "freedom" from his affliction. Support for this interpretation is also drawn from two biblical verses: "Small and great alike are there [in the grave] and the slave is free [*chofshi*] of his master" (Job 3:19), and: "abandoned [*chofshi*] among the dead, like bodies lying in the grave" (Psalms 88:6).

Both interpretations take it to be the designation for a leprosarium, which is also consistent with the rabbinic declaration: "Four [in life] are regarded as though they were dead": the destitute, the blind, the childless, and the leper (BT *Nedarim* 64b).

* As noted above (chapter 5), leprosy, a skin affliction known as Hansen's disease, is not identical with the biblical *tzara'at*, which was incurred on account of sin, was not contagious, and required a *kohen*, rather than a physician, to remove.

2 Kings 16

Details Details — When the Sources Differ: Triangulating the Biblical Reality

It is high time to discuss the fact that the Book of Kings is not our only biblical source for the history of the Judean and Samarian monarchies. There is also the Book of Chronicles. In most cases, the narratives of these two books differ largely in their perspectives (we will have more to say about this when we reach Chronicles), but occasionally—as in the case of this chapter—they differ in their recitation of the facts as well.

According to our chapter, Ahaz, King of Judah, "followed the ways of the kings of Israel. He even consigned (*he'evir*) his *son* to the fire, in the abhorrent fashion of the nations which the Lord had dispossessed before the Israelites" (3). Chronicles, however, reports that "he made offerings in the Valley of Ben-hinnom and burned (*va-yav'er*) his *sons* in fire" (2 Chron. 28:3). Which was it: one son or many sons?

Malbim, ever intent upon preserving the literal integrity of Scripture, noted that there is a distinction between burning something and consigning it to the flames— the former suggesting the possibility of partial burning and the latter implying its total consumption. Hence, we may infer that Ahaz had placed more than one son into the fire, one of whom was completely consumed while the other(s) emerged yet alive. Indeed, the Talmud stipulates that "Hezekiah's father [i.e., Ahaz] sought to do so to him, but his mother protected him as a salamander" (BT *Sanhedrin* 63b), which, according to rabbinic lore, was fireproof.

Furthermore, whereas Kings reports that the coalition of Aram and Israel "besieged Ahaz but could not overcome [him]" (5), Chronicles states explicitly that Aram "defeated him and took many of his men captive" (2 Chron. 28:5). In this case, we have a third biblical source, the Book of Isaiah, which seems to side with Kings, stating that the coalition "marched upon Jerusalem to attack it; but they were not able to attack it" (Isaiah 7:1). Malbim saw the two versions as congruent, explaining that whereas Jerusalem withstood assault, an initial, successful, Aramean attack took place elsewhere in Judah.

We shall shortly (chapter 18, and Isaiah 36, as well) have another occasion to compare these three biblical sources in the matter of Sennacherib's invasion.

SECOND KINGS

2 Kings 17

From Samaria to Samaritans
Converts, Yes — But Was Their Conversion Sincere?

After a three-year siege, Samaria fell to the Assyrian king Shalmaneser. Our chapter records its fall in the following words:

> In the ninth year of Hoshea [ben Elah], the king of Assyria captured Samaria. He deported the Israelites to Assyria and settled them in Halah, at the [River] Habor, at the River Gozan, and in the towns of Media. (17:6)

Following their characteristic practice of transferring populations (which diversified their empire and punished rebellious tributaries while also forestalling potential rebellion), the Assyrians then took people who were indigenous to those locations and resettled them in Samaria, where "they did not worship the Lord; so the Lord sent lions against them which killed some of them" (25). Their interpretation of this event was that they "do not know the rules of the God of the land" (26), whereupon the king had some of the land's former priests returned there to instruct them in those "rules." The result was a syncretistic form of worship described as "They worshiped the Lord, while serving their own gods according to the practices of the nations from which they had been deported" (33).

These, then, were the people who came to be known, during the Second Temple period, as Samaritans, as in the New Testament's "Good Samaritan," after whom a famous law is named that provides legal protection to someone who provides assistance to a person who is injured or in danger. Their descendants, still called Samaritans, live in

Nablus, in proximity to ancient Samaria, and worship in a temple atop Mt. Gerizim.

The Sages of the Talmud, however, were wont to refer to them as Kutheans (*Kutiyim*) on account of their place of origin (24) and debated whether their worship of the Lord was a sincere religious conversion (*gerei tzedek*) or motivated by fear. Their conclusion was that they were *gerei arayot*—converts on account of the lions (i.e., converted from fear)—and not to be regarded as Jewish.

2 Kings 18

A Chip off the Davidic Block
But Still Impotent in the Face of the Assyrian Threat?

In Hezekiah, we finally have a worthy successor to King David. He did "what was pleasing to the Lord" (3), "he abolished the shrines" (4), i.e., the platforms (*bamot*) that had been the bane of every other king's existence (as we have been regularly observing), and he even shattered Moses's bronze serpent (see Numbers 21:9), which had become an object of worship. In brief, "He trusted only in the Lord the God of Israel; there was none like him among all the kings of Judah after him, nor among those before him" (5).

God, in turn, "was always with him" (7), this likely emboldening Hezekiah to rebel against the Assyrians. To his misfortune, however, this occurred while the Assyrians were besieging Samaria on account of its failure to submit to their rule. The result was that as soon as they exiled the ten northern tribes to places in Asia Minor, they were free to turn their attention to the recalcitrant Judeans.

Hence, "In the fourteenth year of King Hezekiah, King Sennacherib of Assyria marched against all the fortified towns of Judah and seized them" (13). Hezekiah, rather than reaffirming his independence, as we might have expected given our introduction, caved in. Not only did he submit to the Assyrian demand for tribute, but in order to meet the payment he cut down the gilded doors and posts of the Temple.

At this point, we would do well to pause and consider the following rabbinic source, compliments of the Mishnah (*Pesahim* 4:9): "Six deeds were performed by Hezekiah King of Judah. Three were acceptable [to the Sages] and three were unacceptable." The aforementioned shattering of the bronze serpent was among the acceptable deeds; cutting down the Temple doors to pay the Assyrian tribute was unacceptable.

In other words, while Hezekiah surpassed his predecessors and successors in his devotion to God, it is likely that they had set such a low standard that exceeding them still left him open to legitimate criticism in other regards and impotent before the Assyrian threat. We shall have occasion to return to this source and this observation anon. (See Isaiah 36–37.)

2 Kings 19

Introducing Isaiah: A New Sort of Prophet

In the previous chapter, we learned that Hezekiah initially met the Assyrian threat with diplomacy. He dispatched a delegation of his chamberlain, scribe, and recorder to meet with an Assyrian officer named Rabshakeh. Of greater curiosity than their actual exchange, however, is the request made by the Judeans: "Please, speak to your servants in Aramaic, for we understand it; do not speak to us in Judean in the hearing of the people on the wall" (26). That Judean noblemen spoke Aramaic—then the *lingua franca* of the Middle East—is not nearly as surprising as the implication that an Assyrian spoke Hebrew.

IN THE COMPANY OF PROPHETS

The Sages thought that unusual enough that they declared him to be an apostate Jew (*Sanhedrin* 60a), whereas Radak observed that "lots of people speak foreign languages" (18:17).

Our chapter picks up at the point that the delegates report their conversation with Rabshakeh to King Hezekiah, who responded by sending them—decked out in sackcloth—to the Prophet Isaiah. The balance of the chapter presents the text of Hezekiah's plea for divine intercession against the Assyrian threat and the Lord's reply—as delivered by Isaiah.

This is not only our introduction to Isaiah, per se, but to classical prophecy itself. In our comments to the Book of Samuel, we had occasion to introduce the term "apostolic" prophecy to describe the activities of such early prophets as Samuel, Nathan, and Gad, whose prophetic function consisted of missions—usually political in nature—that they undertook at God's behest. (See our "Samuel in Retrospect.") These matter-of-fact activities were conducted and reported in ordinary prosaic terms, as distinct from the activities of such later prophets as Isaiah, Jeremiah, and Ezekiel, whose prophecies were religious in nature and were delivered in poetic, even lyrical, terms that we often find obscure, even impenetrable.

The Isaiah of our chapter appears as both a prophet and as an actor in an ongoing historical event. That distinction may make it easier for us to parse our chapter (and the contents of the Book of Isaiah) to distinguish between what he said as a divine emissary and what he spoke on his own recognizance.

SECOND KINGS

2 Kings 20

The Vicissitudes of Hezekiah

And Why the Bizarre Show-and-Tell with the Babylonians?

In this chapter, Hezekiah experienced some notable ups and downs. First, he became critically ill. Then, after he recited what, to all appearances, was a very brief prayer (it takes up barely two thirds of v. 3), Isaiah returned to forecast his recovery and that God would even grant him 15 extra years. So far, so good. But then, Hezekiah asked the prophet to provide a sign to establish the credibility of his prediction, which seemed to jeopardize his situation by giving an indication that his faith was somehow imperfect. However, the prophet acceded to his request and even granted him his choice of signs, which was realized in practice ("let the shadow recede ten degrees" 10–11).

So far, so good—again. But then, the Babylonians made their initial appearance as an up-and-coming world power and presented Hezekiah with yet another challenge. After receiving a Babylonian delegation bearing him a gift, Hezekiah took them on a tour of all the treasuries and storehouses in his kingdom (which must have been replenished since he emptied them in tribute to Assyria in Chapter 18). One can easily imagine how the Judean king, ruling over a very small territory, was captivated by the attention shown him by the Babylonian king and reciprocated by proudly showing off his own wealth and importance.

Then, Isaiah made yet another appearance and rebuked Hezekiah for his extravagant openness and predicted that those same Babylonians would empty those treasuries and take his royal descendants captive, as, in fact, they eventually did. The chapter closes with a somewhat oblique statement: "Hezekiah declared to Isaiah, 'The word of the Lord that you have spoken is good.' For he thought, it meant that safety is assured for my time" (19). Once again, we are challenged to determine whether this statement—as in the case of the receding shade—is a self-serving attempt by Hezekiah to set the terms of his own destiny.

2 Kings 21

He Who Forgets — Shall Be Forgotten

But Most of Manasseh's Many Sins Were Not Exactly the Result of Absent-Mindedness

Manasseh, who succeeded Hezekiah, was his father's opposite in many ways. As constant and comprehensive as Hezekiah's loyalty was to God, so was Manasseh's inclination to revert to the worst practices of his predecessors—typified here by reference to King Ahab and to the ubiquitous high places (*bamot*) whose allure only Hezekiah had been able to withstand (3). Indeed, his very name—derived from the verbal root N-Sh-H, "to forget" (see Gen. 41:51)—personifies his neglect of God and His ways. The Mishnah (*Sanhedrin* 10:1–2) declares that he is one of the three Israelite kings who has no share in the world to come, and yet his reign of 55 years exceeded that of any other king of either Judah or Samaria.

A particularly striking feature of the bill of particulars submitted about Manasseh is contained in verse 6: "He consigned his son to the fire; he practiced soothsaying (*'onen*) and divination (*nichesh*), and consulted ghosts (*'ob*) and familiar spirits (*yid'onim*); he did much that was displeasing to the Lord, to vex Him." This recalls Deut. 18:10: "Let no one be found among you who consigns his son or daughter to the fire, or who is an augur, a soothsayer (*me'onen*), a diviner (*menahesh*), a sorcerer." One gets the impression that Manasseh made a point of locating cardinal prohibitions in the Torah and deliberately violating them.

Because the people followed Manasseh, "Therefore the Lord spoke through His servants the prophets" (10) to rebuke them. Under the reasonable assumption that if Isaiah had been one of those prophets he would have been named, the Sages—in *Seder Olam*, a work of rabbinic chronology—speculated on the identities of these anonymous prophets, naming them as Joel, Nahum, and Habakuk. Curiously, the biblical records of their prophecies do not connect them to the reign of any particular king, as it does for other prophets, so how can the rabbinic speculation be sustained? According to this tradition, so reprehensible was Manasseh that his very name was omitted from the historical record in a kind of quid pro quo: He was forgetful of God, so the Bible overlooked him.

2 Kings 22

Good King Josiah and the Scroll of the Law
Traditional vs. Critical Understandings

Our chapter has become part of the stock-in-trade of biblical criticism. According to the prevalent theory of the multiple authorship of the Torah (the Documentary Hypothesis), the scroll of the Law that was recovered during the restoration of the Temple under King Josiah was none other than the Book of Deuteronomy making its first appearance. By reviewing the pertinent text, we may see how both sides to this issue interpret it.

> Then the high priest Hilkiah said to the scribe Shaphan, "I have found a scroll of the Teaching (Law, *Sefer ha-Torah*) in

the House of the Lord." And Hilkiah gave the scroll to Shaphan, who read it. The scribe Shaphan then went to the king and reported to the king... "The high priest Hilkiah has given me a scroll"; and Shaphan read it to the king. When the king heard the words of the scroll of the Teaching, he rent his clothes (8–11).

And the king ordered: "Go, inquire of the Lord on my behalf, and on behalf of the people, and on behalf of all Judah, concerning the words of this scroll that has been found. For great indeed must be the wrath of the Lord that has been kindled against us, because our fathers did not obey the words of this scroll to do all that has been prescribed for us" (12–13).

The critical view posits that had the scroll been just a copy of an existing Torah, it would not have evoked such a response on the parts of the king and the people. Ergo, it was a discovery more than a recovery.

Not surprisingly, the unusual impact of the scroll did not escape notice by rabbinic interpreters, who had alternate explanations for it. One such commentary, cited by Radak, takes note of the fact that Josiah's reign was preceded by the 55-year reign of Manasseh, during which Torah law was calculatingly neglected and, arguably, copies of the Torah were removed from circulation. To Josiah and his contemporaries, then, it was as though the Torah had been given anew. Another viewpoint, that of Malbim, relies on the parallel description of this event in 2 Chronicles, in which the scroll is called "a scroll of the Lord's teaching given by Moses" (34:9), which is interpreted to mean that it was the original Torah text in Moses's own handwriting. Hence, its recovery was met with such pathos and dedication.

In response to a critical claim that Deuteronomy could not have existed until Josiah's era because of the recurring references in Kings to the worship at *bamot* (high places)—prohibited by Deuteronomic law (12:5, 16:6), Joseph Hertz, Chief Rabbi of the British Commonwealth (1872–1946), wrote:

It is the old familiar argument that the Law could not have existed because it can be shown that it was broken! According to such logic, there could never have been any Prohibition Law in America (*The Pentateuch and Haftorahs* London: Soncino, 1960, 940).

2 Kings 23

A Who's Who of Ancient Idolatry — And an Interesting Sympathetic Treatment of the *Bamot* (High Places)

Our chapter spares no detail in describing the efforts of King Josiah to eliminate all vestiges of idolatry from his kingdom; so much so, in fact, that it reads like a "Who's Who" of ancient Near Eastern religions. Here's a sampling:

- "All the objects made for Baal and Asherah and all the host of heaven... the sun and moon and constellations" (4–5);
- "Topheth, which is in the Valley of Ben-Hinnom, so that no one might consign his son or daughter to the fire of Molech" (10);
- "The shrines (*bamot*) facing Jerusalem... which King Solomon of Israel had built for Ashtoreth, the abomination of the Sidonians, for Chemosh, the abomination of Moab, and for Milcom, the detestable thing of the Ammonites" (13);
- "The altar in Bethel [and] the shrine (*bamah*) made by Jeroboam son of Nebat" (15);
- "All the cult places (*bamot*) in the towns of Samaria" (19).

Gersonides (Ralbag) addressed the attribution of "shrines" to Solomon, observing that they were introduced by Solomon's foreign wives (see 1 Kings 11:1ff.), but were ascribed to him because he tolerated them. Radak was troubled by the failure of several of Josiah's righteous predecessors (e.g., Asa and Jehoshaphat) to remove the idols and intimated that their tolerance of the *bamot* was nigh idolatrous.

We ought to note that while the other forms of worship listed here are clearly idolatrous, *bamot* (high places), prohibited once the Temple was established, might not have been so bad. In this regard, a most unusual interpretation of the *bamot* was offered by the Netziv (R. Naftali Tzvi Yehudah Berlin, 1816–1893), who presumed that they were born of an irresistible, yet positive, impulse to serve God. After Jeroboam prohibited pilgrimage to Jerusalem and established the golden calves in Dan and Beersheba, people could not reconcile themselves to never again sacrificing to God. Hence, in conscious violation of strict Torah law, they persisted to worship God at the *bamot*. The Netziv likened their behavior to that of the 250 elders who mimicked Aaron's offering of incense (Numbers 16–17)—knowing fully well that it would cost them their lives—because they could not resist the impulse to be so close to God. (Commentary on Shir HaShirim 6:5.)

2 Kings 24

The Pre-Exile of Jehoiachin and a Significant Name-Change for Mataniah — Zedekiah

The Babylonians, who first entered the region during the reign of Hezekiah, now asserted themselves and subjugated Judah, whose attempted rebellion was suppressed by the combined forces of "Chaldeans, Arameans, Moabites, and Ammonites" (2), in punishment for the crimes committed by Manasseh.

Only three months into the reign of Jehoiachin, Nebuchadnezzar besieged Jerusalem, but Jehoiachin did not capitulate until the eighth year of his reign (or the seventh, as per Jeremiah 52:28)—implying that he withstood the pressure for 8 years, which was no mean feat. The royal family was exiled and the treasures of both palace and Temple were taken, including "the golden decorations in the Temple of the Lord, which King Solomon of Israel had made, as the Lord had warned" (13), a reference to 20:17: "A time is coming when everything in your palace which your ancestors have stored up to this day will be carried off to Babylon; nothing will remain behind, said the Lord."

Along with the royal family, the Babylonians exiled Jerusalem's upper class, leaving behind "only the poorest of the peasantry" (14). Nebuchadnezzar set up a vassal king in Jehoiachin's stead—his uncle Mataniah, "changing his name to Zedekiah" (17). What was the purpose of the name change? Mataniah means "gift of God" and Zedekiah means "justice of God." According to several of the medieval exegetes (Rashi, Kara, Radak), the change was intended by Nebuchadnezzar to convey the message to Zedekiah that God would deal with him justly if he were to rebel.

2 Kings 25

A Silver Lining? — And the Establishment of a Model of Jewish Leadership for the Ages

If Nebuchadnezzar thought that the "gift of God" (Mataniah) persona would embolden Zedekiah (see chapter 24), he was right. After nine years of rebellion, the Babylonians returned to Jerusalem, besieged it for two years, and, having brought the population to starvation, breached the walls and put the city—Temple and palaces alike—to the torch.

Once again, the Temple vessels and furnishings were looted (implying that they had been restored or replaced after their earlier looting in Chapter 24). Those that could be carried off to Babylonia were taken there, while those that could not be transported intact—like the bronze pillars, stands, and tank (13)—were broken up and carried off piecemeal. Zedekiah paid a dear price for his rebelliousness: his own sons were killed in his presence and then he was blinded. The high priest, his deputy, and three official gatekeepers of the Temple were executed, along with the captain of the guard and other military officers (18ff.).

Again (see 24:14), only the upper class was exiled; the most impoverished of the population were left behind "to be vinedressers and field hands" (12). To govern them, Nebuchadnezzar appointed Gedaliah, son of Ahikam, son of Shafan, the latter two having been members of the delegation dispatched by King Josiah to inquire of the prophetess Hulda when the scroll of the law was discovered (2 Kings 22:12, 14). From a parallel passage in Jeremiah, we also learn that Ahikam had defended that prophet from the mob that sought his death (26:24).

Since Jeremiah had counseled capitulation to Babylonia (which is why the mob wanted to lynch him), he was likely viewed favorably by Nebuchadnezzar, and the appointment of Ahikam's son may therefore have been a politically safe one. Indeed, the only words of his that have been recorded in the Bible are "Stay in the land and serve the king of Babylon, and it will go well with you" (24). Gedaliah did not last long. He was assassinated by survivors of the royal family (hence the Fast of Gedaliah) and the remaining Judeans fled to Egypt in fear of Babylonian reprisal.

On the other hand, the Book of Kings ends on a somewhat positive note: Nebuchadnezzar's son and successor eventually released the exiled King Jehoiachin from prison (27), elevated him to the highest ranks of Babylonian nobility (28), and provided for his lifetime maintenance (29). According to later Jewish sources, the descendants of Jehoiachin became the exilarchs (*Rashei Golah*), empowered by the Babylonians—and, later, the Persians, Medes, Greeks, Byzantines, and Muslims—to oversee whatever self-rule the Jews of Babylonia were granted by their overlords. Even the family of the patriarch (*Nasi*), who served a similar function in the Land of Israel, acknowledged the superiority of the exilarchs on account of their more direct descent from the Davidic kings, and the Sabbath morning liturgical passage called *Yekum Purkan* ("May Deliverance Arise") still bestows blessings on the *Resh Galuta*, as he was called in Aramaic.

IN THE COMPANY OF PROPHETS

Kings and
Early Prophets in Retrospect

The Talmud, employing hyperbole, stipulates: "Israel had many prophets; twice the number of those who left Egypt," which, even limiting ourselves to the 600,000 males above the age of 20, would surpass one million! Where, then, are their prophecies? "Rather, a prophecy that was needed for all generations was recorded, while one that was not so needed was not recorded" (*Megillah* 14a).

In a succinct, but seminal essay on this assertion, the historian Avraham Grossman acknowledged: "The fact that it is not always simple to reveal this lesson [i.e., why an historical event was recorded] should not discourage us from the attempt and effort to uncover it. Avoiding it is tantamount to falsifying a sacred task" ("The Use of Historical Background in Teaching Early Prophets," *Maayanot* vol. 11 (1985), 291). He then added: "Three important tools can assist us in our search for these lessons: rabbinic Midrash, literary-aesthetic means (expansion, emphasis, leading words, etc.), and the historical background" (ibid.).

If we were to honor his instructions and make that attempt, what might we conclude about any, let alone all, of the prophecies preserved in the books we have reflected on here?

First, we need to bear in mind the distinction we have drawn on more than one occasion between the political and social missions undertaken by such "Early" Prophets as Samuel, Nathan, Elijah, and Elisha that some scholars have designated "apostolic," and literary prophecy that is more the provenance of the "Later" Prophets (Isaiah, Jeremiah, Ezekiel, etc.). I would submit that the challenge to find a relevant lasting message in the prophetic record of a specific historical event is greater than locating it in a classic prophetic speech.

If you agree with this proposition, then you will appreciate that we have now completed the hermeneutic circle and returned to the closing paragraph of the introduction to this book. There I retold the anecdote about the dean of the Vienna Rabbinical Seminary who, when asked to identify the best commentary on the Bible, replied, without hesitation: "Jewish History." Once again I leave you to ponder.

www.ingramcontent.com/pod-product-compliance
Lightning Source LLC
Chambersburg PA
CBHW052100280426
43673CB00070B/31